# COMPARATIVE CHRISTIANITY

# COMPARATIVE CHRISTIANITY
## A STUDENT'S GUIDE TO A RELIGION AND ITS DIVERSE TRADITIONS

## THOMAS A. RUSSELL

Universal-Publishers
Boca Raton

*Comparative Christianity: A Student's Guide to a Religion and its Diverse Traditions*

Universal-Publishers
Boca Raton, Florida • USA
2010

ISBN-10: 1-59942-877-6
ISBN-13: 978-1-59942-877-2

www.universal-publishers.com


Library of Congress Cataloging-in-Publication Data

Russell, Thomas Arthur, 1954-
Comparative Christianity : a student's guide to a religion and its diverse
traditions / Thomas A. Russell.
    p. cm.
Includes bibliographical references and index.
ISBN-13: 978-1-59942-877-2 (pbk. : alk. paper)
ISBN-10: 1-59942-877-6 (pbk. : alk. paper)
1. Christianity. I. Title.
BR121.3.R88 2010
230--dc22
                                        2009054265

# TABLE OF CONTENTS
✠

# PREFACE

✠

Christianity! Why in the world do we need yet another book on that subject anyway?

Christianity is the largest religion in the world. Christianity has over two billion members worldwide with many different expressions of beliefs, ways of living, ceremonies, and institutions: the Amish with horse and buggies, Pentecostals who speak in tongues, Ethiopian Orthodox who claim to have the original Ark of the Covenant, and Roman Catholics with the beautiful Sistine Chapel.

After teaching comparative Christianity in stand-alone courses or in comparative religion courses for over 20 years, I have come to the conclusion that students do not know much about Christianity. Either they are practicing believers who feel their own faith is the only version of Christianity or they have no connections with Christianity and know nothing at all about it.

As a result, a new basic introduction to Christianity was needed that could make up for this deficit.

This book attempts to remedy this situation by acquainting students with Christianity and its subgroups.

Choosing who to include is a difficult task in itself. Three approaches can be taken. First, pick 1 Christian group to represent the rest. Second, limit choices to those groups which are seen as legitimately Christian by the majority of Christian bodies in existence today. Third, possibly include any group that claims connections to Christianity, whether or not it adheres to commonly accepted beliefs of the tradition or whether it is recognized as Christian by the majority of existing Christian communities. This approach includes those groups which began in the Christian environment, but have moved to their own unique place outside the norms of the tradition. This book uses the third method.

To carry this out, the text first explores what Christians have in common and then works through the three major subdivisions of the faith, Eastern, Roman, and Protestant Christianity. Using categories common to many definitions of religion, each chapter employs the following categories: beliefs, individual and group moral codes, ceremonies, and associations.[1]

---

[1] Many definitions of the term "religion" use these categories. For examples, see http://www.religioustolerance.org/rel_defn.htm, http://www.religioustolerance.org /rel_defn.htm and http://www.thefreedictionary.com/religion. Two authors have

Beliefs refer to the concepts or ideas of a religion, such as who is God or what happens at death. Individual or group moral codes explore how a religion impacts daily living. For example, does it dictate or suggest how a believer should relate to members of the opposite sex in clothing and activities? Ceremonies explore rituals, both individual and community, that are significant for each group. This discussion includes which ceremonies are performed and what meaning is ascribed to them by the faithful. Finally, associations refer to how a religious community is organized and deals with types of structures for running the group and leadership selection and roles.

Taken together, these four categories give a broadly conceived picture of a particular Christian community. If only one category is explored, little would be known about that community. For example, since students know I teach comparative religions, many will come up to me and ask, "Dr. Russell, what do the Mormons, Roman Catholics, or Jehovah's Witnesses believe?" With great restraint I normally say something like, "You can't really know a religion if you only know their beliefs!" I then add, "You need to know about how they live, what rituals they carry out, and how they are organized."

Each chapter provides many details. Because over the years students have asked about particular groups, I have added more detail about some of these (i.e., the Amish, the Coptic, and the Ethiopian Orthodox churches). Each chapter also includes review questions.

I would like to thank those who have supported my efforts. First, I appreciate the support of several institutions: the University of Memphis, Western Kentucky University, and Belmont University. All have given me the opportunity to teach Comparative Christianity and each have colleagues who have supported me in the teaching and writing process. I owe a large debt of gratitude to Harvard University's Pluralism Project and the Louisville Institute for the three grants given me that have supported my research. Armed with their money, I have had the time to observe religious services and meet community members of many of these faiths. A big thanks to all my students who have used earlier versions of this book (over 1,000 students in 10 years) and who have contributed their suggestions for added materials. I wish to offer my gratitude to members of many of these communities of faith who have willingly opened their hearts and shared their faith with me. I want to express my thanks to my mother, Elizabeth Russell Fullerton, who died just recently. Her constant question, "When will your book be published?" pushed me ever onward to completion. Finally, and most important, I offer special thanks to my wife, Anne, and my son and his wife, Thomas and

---

provided excellent examples of the use of these four categories when defining the term religion: Ronald L. Johnstone and Julia Corbett Hemeyer. See Ronald L. Johnstone, *Religion in Society*, 8th ed. (Upper Saddle River, NJ: Pearson/Prentice-Hall, 2007) and Julia Corbett Hemeyer, *Religion in America*, 6th edition (Upper Saddle River, NJ: Prentice-Hall, 2009).

Stephanie, for their support. Stephanie deserves a special acknowledgement because as a professional graphic artist, she designed the cover for the book.

Hopefully, after using this book, students will understand their neighbors and co-workers a bit more and armed with that fresh understanding, they can foster better community relationships and a better world.

# CHAPTER I
✠
# INTRODUCTION TO CHRISTIANITY

## Introduction

Christianity is the largest religion in the world with two billion plus followers found on every continent.[1] Three large movements comprise the Christian movement today: Eastern Christianity, Roman Catholic Christianity, and Protestant Christianity. Followers of Christianity are called Christians.[2]

Succinctly stated, Christians are men and women who place their trust (i.e., faith) in Jesus Christ as Savior and Lord. Savior refers to the belief that Jesus saves people from their entrapment in sin and Lord means something akin to "boss."

*Christ*, the title given to Jesus, is the basis for this religion's label, Christianity. This term is derived from the Greek word "christos," which means "anointed." The Hebrew word for anointed is "mashiah," hence the English word, "messiah."

## Beliefs: Religious Texts

Jesus wrote nothing of his own. Instead, the Christian community bases its beliefs and practices on the Hebrew Scriptures (Genesis to Malachi), which they call the Old Testament and the New Testament (Matthew to Revelation). The Old Testament is written in Hebrew, except for bits of Aramaic.

---

[1] 33% of the world's population is Christian, 22% Muslim, 15% Hindu, 14% non-religious, 6% Buddhist, and .5% Jewish.

Current Christian growth is fastest in developing nations in Africa, Asia, and Latin America. For more details, see John Philip Jenkins, *The Next Christendom: The Coming of Global Christianity* (Oxford: Oxford University Press, 2002).

[2] Followers of Christ were first called Christians or "Christ-ones" at Antioch, Syria in the 40s CE in Acts 11:26.

The New Testament is primarily written in *Koiné Greek*, which means "common" or "street" Greek. This was the language of everyday life. Taken together these collections are called the Bible.

Some Christians add other books. A majority of this extra material comes from a collection called the *Apocrypha*. The Apocrypha was mostly written by anonymous Jews living outside of Palestine after the Hebrew Bible was completed, but before the New Testament was penned. Because of this, this collection is sometimes referred to as Intertestamental Literature. Apocryphal texts include:

> 1 and 2 Esdras, Additions to Esther, Judith, Tobit, 1 and 2 Maccabees, Prayer of Manasseh, Ecclesiasticus, Baruch, Letter to Jeremiah, Prayer of Azariah and the Song of Three Jews, Susanna, Bel and the Dragon and The Wisdom of Solomon. [3]

Jews used the Apocrypha in the distant past, but do not use it now. According to questionable tradition, it was dropped in 90 CE at a meeting at Yavneh (Jamnia). The Christian community has been split from its earliest years over the inclusion of the Apocrypha in Bibles. Early church leaders, such as Augustine, Cyprian, and Clement, had Bibles that contained the Apocrypha because they used the *Septuagint* as a basis for the Old Testament. The Septuagint was the first Greek translation of the Hebrew Scriptures, 250 BCE, and it included the Apocrypha. However, other early church leaders followed the Jewish tradition and did not retain them (Origen, Cyril, and Jerome).

Today Catholics and Eastern Christians include the Apocrypha and consider them to be equal to Genesis to Revelation (Roman Catholics call them Deuterocanonical Literature). The former decided this in 1546 CE at the Council of Trent and the Eastern tradition uses a variety of extra books depending on the specific community.

Protestants have either retained the Roman Apocrypha or dropped the material altogether. Martin Luther incorporated these into his 1534 German translation of the Bible, but added that although they were not equal to the

---

[3] Eastern Christianity adds different texts depending on which community is examined. For example, the Ethiopian Orthodox Church has 81 books in its canon. For more information, see Chapter Three.

Intertestamental literature also includes another collection of Jewish books, which have never been part of canon and this is called the Pseudepigrapha. These were written in Hebrew, Aramaic, and Greek between 200 BCE and 200 CE. They are apocalypses, legendary histories, psalms, and wisdom literature. Some are ascribed to famous people, such as Enoch, Adam, Moses, and Isaiah. Some of these books include: 1 Enoch, The Book of Jubilees, Testaments of the Twelve Patriarchs, Psalms of Solomon, Assumption of Moses, the Letter of Aristeas, and 3rd and 4th Maccabees.

rest of the Bible, they were nevertheless "profitable and good to read." Thanks to him, some Protestants use them for teaching, but do not see them as scripture. Other Protestants explicitly rejected the inspiration, authority, and spiritual usefulness of the Apocrypha.

Bible books were determined to be part of the official collection or canon for different reasons. According to questionable tradition, the Jewish portion was determined as a by-product of the Council of Jamnia in 90 CE when only books originally written in Hebrew and written before the "Silent Period" began were included.[4] The Christian portion (or the New Testament) used three criteria for acceptance:

- Did an original apostle or Paul write the book? This gave the book a ring of authenticity and authority.
- Did the book have widespread use in the ancient Christian community? The more the book was used in the ancient Christian community, the more it was accepted.
- Did the content of the book agree with what was commonly held as orthodox? If it did, it was accepted. If not, the book was rejected for the New Testament.

What Christians call the Old Testament (in opposition to the New Covenant initiated by Jesus Christ) is the Hebrew *TANAK*. The TANAK includes three sections: the Pentateuch or first five books (Genesis through Deuteronomy), the Prophets (an extensive collection from Joshua to Malachi) and the Writings (books such as Proverbs and Psalms).

The New Testament can be divided into two sections: the four Gospels and Acts through Revelation. The most important sources about the life and mission of Jesus are the four Gospels: Matthew, Mark, Luke, and John. The first three are called the Synoptics because they "have a common view." The Gospels are selective histories of the life, death, and resurrection of Jesus Christ. None intends to tell everything. Instead, the authors only include what they believe is important for their readers. Acts through Revelation contain three types of literature: history (Acts), letters, and an apocalypse (Revelation). Like the Gospels, the Book of Acts is a selective portrayal of the developments in the earliest years of the Christian faith as it spread from Palestine to Asia Minor, Greece, and Rome. The first part of the book deals with the Apostle Peter, while the second section focuses on the Apostle Paul. New Testament letters were written by several authors to a variety of churches and individuals. They were either responses to specific situations or problems in the church or they were general letters with wide-ranging content. These

---

[4] The "Silent Period" refers to the end of the Jewish prophetic line, which occurred after 450 BCE.

letters were written to churches or individuals. Revelation is an apocalyptic work, filled with symbols (i.e., 666), climactic battles (i.e., Armageddon), and visions of heaven, earth, and judgment.

### Beliefs: Religious Tradition

*Religious tradition* may be defined as anything a community of faith writes or pronounces outside of the foundational religious texts. This category includes hymns, prayers, sermons, theological and devotional writings, and canon or church law or organizational rules.

Christians maintain three distinct views on how to handle tradition in relation to the Bible. In other words, what is (are) the final authorities used to determine beliefs and practices?

Eastern Christians maintain that the Bible and the tradition of the church until 1054 CE when Eastern and Western Christianity went separate ways are equal authorities. Roman Catholicism teaches that the Bible and the tradition of the church until this very moment are equal authorities. Finally, Protestantism believes that the Bible is the sole authority with tradition playing a secondary, informative role.

To better understand these distinctions, it is advisable to examine a specific example: Purgatory. Purgatory is the belief that at death Christians may go to another destination rather than heaven or hell. Some believers may need to go to Purgatory for further cleansing and preparation prior to entering heaven.

If a person says, "Where is this doctrine found in the Bible and/or the first 1,000 years of Christian tradition?" they are thinking like an Eastern Christian. If they ask, "Where is this doctrine taught in the Bible and/or by church tradition up until this moment?" they are thinking like a Roman Catholic. If an individual says, "Where is this doctrine taught in the Bible?" they are thinking like a Protestant.

### Beliefs: Other Foundations

Christianity begins with the life of Jesus, a Jew living in Roman times. There was a time when arguments against his existence were made with credibility.[5] However, that position has little respect today.

---

[5] Examples of scholars and historians who have argued against the existence of Jesus as an actual historical figure include: Constantin-Francois Volney, Charles Francois Dupuis, Bruno Bauer, George Albert Wells, Earl Doherty, and Robert M. Price. Specific arguments put forth have been: the lack of eyewitnesses, a lack of archaeological evidence, the absence of Jesus in ancient written materials, and the notion that Jesus is actually a mix of ancient mythologies. For a summary, see Will Durant, *Caesar and Christ: A History of Roman Civilization and of Christianity from Their Beginnings to A. D. 337*, Volume 3 (New York: Simon and Schuster, 1944).

Instead, arguments about Jesus swirl around what he said and did. Did he claim divinity for himself and did he perform miracles? Were apparent claims to divinity or assertions that he performed miracles merely added by the early church to enhance the new faith's credibility?

This all goes back to a person's presuppositions about the veracity of the biblical text and assumptions about the viability of miraculous events (see later for the debate between traditionalists and modernists).

The biblical texts *say* or *suggest* the following about Jesus:

- He was born between 7 and 3 BCE in Bethlehem, Judea.
- He grew up in Nazareth as a Jew.
- He began his formal ministry when baptized by John the Baptist.
- He gathered disciples.
- He taught about the Kingdom of God, often using parables.
- His teachings put him in direct conflict with the Jewish establishment.
- He suffered and then died on the cross at the hands of the Romans, encouraged by Jewish leaders, probably for the crime of sedition.
- He claimed to be the Son of Man, the Son of God, and Messiah.
- He rose from the dead.
- He ascended into heaven.
- He promised to return one day.

From its beginning, the Christian community created statements of beliefs and practices for the devout called *Creeds*. Not only do they serve as summaries of what early Christians thought, but also they are a helpful way of understanding Christianity. Today, certain Christian groups repeat these regularly in their services, while others never use them. In either case, the majority of Christians agree on what is being said.

For hundreds of years, Christians believed that the 12 original apostles penned the creed that bears their name, *The Apostles' Creed*. It was thought that each of the original 12 contributed one statement individually. Today, practically all scholars assume that this story is factitious. That being said, many consider the creed to have been influenced by these individuals because it is in fundamental agreement with their ideas. The fullest form of the Apostles' Creed seems to have appeared around 700 CE; however, sections of the creed come from earlier documents with the most significant being the Old Roman Creed. This probably originated in the second half of the second century and may have been used by those about to experience baptism. The Apostles' Creed states:

I believe in God, the Father Almighty, the Maker of Heaven and Earth.
And in Jesus Christ, His only Son, our Lord,
Who was conceived by the Holy Ghost,
Born of the Virgin Mary,
Suffered under Pontius Pilate,
Was crucified, died and buried.
He descended into hell.[6]
The third day He rose again from the dead.
He ascended into heaven,
And sits on the right hand of God, the Father Almighty.
From there he shall come to judge the living and the dead

I believe in the Holy Spirit;
The holy catholic church,
The communion of saints,
The forgiveness of sins,
The resurrection of the dead,
And the life everlasting.

The Apostles' Creed contains:

- Statements about God
- Statements about Jesus Christ
- Statements about the Holy Spirit
- Statements on miscellaneous topics

The Creed contains two short sections. First, there is one God, who is traditionally captured in the masculine term "Father." This God is an all-powerful living spirit who created everything. In the second short section, the Apostles' Creed simply affirms belief in the Holy Spirit.

In the lengthiest section of the Creed, several statements are made about Jesus. These fill out his resume in terms of his person (who he was), and his actions (his birth, death, resurrection, ascension, and future return). He is God the Father's only Son and a believer's Lord or boss. He was conceived and birthed in unique ways (the first by the Holy Spirit, not a human male, and the second, through a virgin mother). Jesus suffered mental and physical anguish during the rule of Pontius Pilate, the Roman procurator, and died on a cross. He rose from the dead on the third day, went up to heaven to be God and will come again to judge all people, living and the dead.

---

[6] The phrase "He descended into hell" refers to the belief that between his death and resurrection, Jesus went to the realm of the dead (see 1 Peter 3:19-20).

The creed's last section contains a set of miscellaneous statements. These say that there is one catholic or universal (not Roman Catholic) church. This church is holy (i.e., separated by God and demonstrating God's righteous character) and composed of believers, living and dead in community. There is forgiveness of sins and a future and final resurrection leading to eternal life. The creed makes no statements about the actual final destination of souls.

The Apostles' Creed points to several crucial Christian beliefs. First, whether the specific community uses the word *Trinity*, Christians believe in the concept. While hard to explain to non-Christians who accuse Christians of polytheism, the Trinity is the belief that God is one essence and yet three persons (Father, Son, and Holy Spirit).

In trying to describe this term, analogy or simile is helpful. The Trinity is like an apple, which is one and yet has constituent parts (core, skin, and meat) or like water, which can be liquid, frozen, or steam.

A second important term is *Incarnation*, in which God became a human being. Third, the *Resurrection* is key to Christian faith. The faithful believe that after three days in the tomb, Jesus rose from the dead in a new spiritual, yet physical or bodily form.

A final idea stemming from the Apostles' Creed has to do with the concept of *Justification by Faith*, a belief that all Christian communities hold in varying forms.

Eastern Christians tend to deemphasize justification compared to Roman Catholicism and Protestantism. The term itself simply means to be pardoned for one's sins. It is intimately tied to a living, dynamic relationship of the sinner to God.

Roman Catholicism has its own view of justification by faith and this view is different than Eastern or Protestant views. The church teaches that justification is a process beginning with initial justification or "being cleansed from sin," continues with progressive justification or "being made righteous," and is consummated with final justification. The former begins with the work of infused grace at baptism and continues with the grace given by the Holy Spirit, through receiving the sacraments and via good works. During a person's lifetime, the faithful Roman Catholic's mind and heart are slowly made more righteous. Final justification occurs after the final judgment, when a righteous person's righteousness will be revealed.

Protestantism believes that justification occurs in a one-time event in which God declares an unrighteous person is righteous because of the work of Jesus. It is given to all who have faith and is seen as God's gift.[7]

---

[7] Roman Catholics and a select group of Protestants have had some significant theological dialogue about the nature and meaning of justification by faith in recent years. A movement called "Evangelicals and Catholics Together" or ECT was established in the 1990s. The group claims to have open, frank discussions of the essentials of Christian truth. According to one of the participants, Chuck Colson, these conversa-

### Christian Ways of Life

Christians are also called *Disciples*, which comes from the same root word as discipline. Being a disciple means that a believer develops an ethical life based on their faith in Jesus Christ. Christians attempt to live by the motto WWJD or "What Would Jesus Do?" Ethics for these disciples use some combination of primary or revelatory sources (i.e., the Bible and tradition) and non-revelatory sources (i.e., the social sciences and philosophy).

Christian lifestyle varies with each Christian group. Some groups set clear guidelines for their members, which they feel best constitutes what the lives of Christians ought to be like. To be a member in good standing of these groups, a person must follow these clearly delineated rules. Some have to do with such issues as dress (i.e., women's jewelry or men's beards) and socialization (i.e., drinking or swimming with members of the opposite sex). Other Christian groups leave the determination of how to live to each member's individual conscience that has been informed somewhat loosely by their interpretation of the Bible and their group's tradition.

---

tions were "not ecumenism in the usual sense of reducing things to the lowest common denominator." See Charles Colson, "Well Done Good and Faithful Servant," *Catholic Exchange* (January 23, 2009), http://catholicexchange.com/2009/01/23/115220/

Colson claims that the Roman Catholic Church has adopted the Protestant view on justification by faith. He says this has been demonstrated by the affirmation of the Protestant view in the 1997 CE document, "The Gift of Salvation," and by Pope Benedict XVI's November 19, 2008 CE comments. In this November 19, 2008 statement, the Pope stated:

> That is why Luther's expression "sola fide" is true if faith is not opposed to charity, to love. Faith is to look at Christ, to entrust oneself to Christ, to be united to Christ, to be conformed to Christ, to his life. And the form, the life of Christ, is love; hence, to believe is to be conformed to Christ and to enter into his love. That is why, in the *Letter to the Galatians*, St. Paul develops above all his doctrine on justification; he speaks of faith that operates through charity (cf. Galatians 5:14). (The Pope is the titular head of the worldwide Roman Catholic Church.) Pope Benedict XVI, "On St. Paul and Justification," see *http://www.zenit.org/article-24302?l=english* (11/19/2008).

In this statement, Pope Benedict remarks that Luther's "faith alone" for justification is true if that faith is linked to charity and love. Believers are justified by faith in Christ and by the actions that flow from one's love for him.

The Pope's statement appears to be simply a reiteration of Roman Catholic views articulated since the Council of Trent in the 1500s CE. However, his speech may also shed light on how differences between certain Protestants and some Roman Catholic theologians are being dealt with on the issue of justification by faith in the early 21st century CE.

## Ceremonies

Christians celebrate rituals alone or in groups. They carry out these in a variety of locations: in homes, in fields, on mountain tops, by river banks, and in buildings commonly called churches.

Church architecture differs from group to group and even within the same group. Three common building styles exist: eastern, western liturgical, and western non-liturgical.[8]

Questions about Christian ceremonies include:

- How many ceremonies are there?
- What names are used for these?
- When are these ceremonies held?
- Who officiates at these ceremonies?
- How are these ceremonies carried out?
- Where are these ceremonies carried out?

## Ceremonies: The Actual Rituals

Ninety-nine percent of Christians have at least two central rituals, that is, rituals that Christians believe Jesus commanded his followers to carry out. The two are some form of *Baptism* and some form of *Communion*. Baptism is a ceremony that marks a person's entrance into the Christian community. The communion ritual remembers Christ's death. Some Christian groups have up to seven ceremonies, but once one moves beyond the first two, there is little agreement about these others. Roman Catholics and Eastern Orthodox Christians add five: confirmation, penance, ordination, marriage, and last rites. Some add foot washing and/or a holy kiss on the cheek of a member of the same sex.

Christians vary on their notions about baptism and communion. While most believe that infants should be baptized, others believe that an individual has to be old enough to know what they believe before they are baptized. Added to this, some believe that baptism should occur during regular church services, while others believe it should occur only at special times. Christians differ on who should do the baptizing—a priest or minister or a friend or family member.

There are a variety of ways by which baptism is carried out. Is water sprinkled or poured on a person's forehead? Perhaps a person is thoroughly submerged in water. Christians differ on how many times a person should be immersed. Some say once, while others say three times to signify the Trinity.

---

[8] See Hinnells, John R., *The New Penguin Handbook of Living Religions, 2nd ed.* (London: Penguin Books, 1998), p. 127 for a drawing of these designs. For definitions of liturgical and non-liturgical, see later in this section of the chapter.

Christians differ on where baptism should take place—in a church in a tank or font or in a creek or a swimming pool.

The diversity in beliefs and practices involving communion is astoundingly wide.[9] The name for the ritual itself varies from group to group. Is this ceremony the Eucharist (i.e., "Thanksgiving"), Holy Communion, or the Lord's Supper?

Groups also disagree about who can take communion. Should it be available to anyone present during the service, members and visitors alike (open communion), to any baptized Christian (modified open communion), to members of a particular faith group no matter where that group is found in the world (closed communion), or to members of the local community only (closed communion)? In the last category, should communion be made available to anyone in the local community or only those in "good standing" (modified closed communion)?

Some Christians believe that anyone from infancy on up can take communion. Others teach that a person must be old enough to understand what they believe before taking communion or that they must have gone through some form of required instruction prior to participation.

Christians disagree over when communion should occur. Should it be at every service, once a month, only a few times a year, or never? Who should officiate at the communion service—the duly designated church official (i.e., the priest) or any member ordained or not? How communion is carried out varies from Christian group to Christian group. Some have members walk up to the front of the church and either kneel or stand to take communion. Others have participants sit in pews or chairs and wait for the communion food and drink to be passed around. Should communion come in one chalice that all share or in individual cups? Christians differ on what should be used. Should wine, grape juice, or water be used? Should unleavened or leavened bread be used or crackers be taken? Should Christians take both elements or just one? If they are taking both, should the elements be given separately or should the bread be mushed into the wine?

### Ceremonies: Three Issues

Three final issues involving Christian ceremonies need to be discussed. First, Christians use two terms to describe their central rituals. These are *Sacrament* and *Ordinance*. Even though rituals may be the same, the terms employed mean two very different things. Of course, there are those groups that use one term when they actually mean the other.

The use of both terms reflects a theological belief about the timing of receiving God's grace (i.e., God's saving and transforming power). In a sacra-

---

[9] Christians use the following Bible verses to teach about Communion: Matthew 26:26-30; Mark 14:22-25; Luke 22:14-23; John 6:48-59 and 13-17; and 1 Corinthians 11:17-34.

ment, a person receives a "zap" of God's grace in the ritual itself. They are "infused" with grace while being baptized or taking communion. An ordinance is a ritual that celebrates grace already received. Grace has already been "imparted" by faith and the ceremony acknowledges that that transaction has already occurred. Thus, in sacramental churches, when a person is baptized they receive a squirt of God's grace (whether or not this actually saves their soul divides sacramental people), while in ordinance churches a person goes through the ordinance of baptism in order to remember the grace that they have already received by being saved.

A second issue concerns the meaning of the ritual (i.e., what actually transpires during these sacraments or ordinances?). In communion, do the elements (i.e., the bread and wine, grape juice, and crackers. etc.) actually become the body and blood of Christ (i.e., Roman Catholicism)?

If they do not become the body and blood, do they have Christ's presence in them? If so, is Christ "in, with, and under" the elements (the Sacramental Union of Lutheranism) or is Christ a "spiritual presence among the people of God" (the Pneumatic Presence of Presbyterianism)?

Finally, if they do not become the body and blood or have Christ's presence in them, do the elements symbolize or represent Christ's body and blood and are taken in remembrance of him (Baptists)?[10]

A final issue involves ceremonial style. Christian churches are either *Liturgical* or *Non-liturgical*. In the former, there is a formatted worship, which members contend has been practiced since the earliest Christian era. Minimal innovation occurs and this maintenance of tradition is highly honored by worshippers. What innovation that does occur normally comes through a group outside the local community. The layout is repeated anywhere in the world where that group worships, regardless of language differences. The precise pattern is often printed in a small book in the pew or in a prayer book. Members and regular attendees seem to know what to do and when to do it, while visitors fumble through the books to keep up. Those who practice liturgical worship find strength and solace in the repetition of style. They find non-liturgical churches too spontaneous and often lacking in things that appeal to them (i.e., "You never know what to expect. Something is lacking"). Roman Catholics, Eastern Christians, Lutheran, and Episcopal Churches are liturgical.

Non-liturgical communities of faith, represented by most Protestants, can pick and choose what elements they want to have in their worship and these selections do not have to be approved by committees outside the local church. These innovations may occur weekly. Non-liturgical Christians are concerned with adjusting worship to fit contemporary times rather than maintaining the style passed down for generations. Those who regularly par-

---

[10] Anglicans can be high or Anglican-Catholic, broad and low or Evangelical church followers depending on their closeness to the Roman Catholic tradition.

ticipate in non-liturgical churches find liturgical churches monotonous and quite boring (i.e., "How can they do the same thing each week?").

Even with the variety found in non-liturgical worship, there may be aspects of worship services that are repeated regularly. This makes many non-liturgical churches quite liturgical.

### *Institutions: History*

Christian institutional history has had several segments each in intervals of 500 years and each division still exists. In the fifth and sixth centuries, what became the *Oriental Christianity* split off from the rest of the faith due to a disagreement over how the human and divine interplays in Jesus.[11] These Christians became the Copts, Ethiopian Orthodox, Armenian, and Thomas Christians of India. A majority of the Christians found in present-day Iraq fit this category.[12]

---

[11] See Chapter Two, "Eastern Christianity."

[12] Although present-day Iraq has a Muslim majority, there are still many Christians living there. However, the statistics on these groups are hard to ascertain and are only estimates. By tradition, the Apostle Thomas established Christianity in the region with the aid of another apostle Addai in the first century CE.

Today, an estimated 600,000 Christians live in Iraq out of 20–22 million total residents or about 3% of the total population. Iraqi Christians can be divided into 3 major groups with 12 subdivisions. Those associated with Rome are in the majority (457,000), non-Roman Catholic, but non-Protestant (152,000), and Protestants (58,000).

The largest group is the Chaldean Catholic Church. Approximately 390,000 members of this body are under the jurisdiction of the Roman Pope and are based in Baghdad. This group has seven bishops and a patriarch, the Patriarch of Babylon. A notable recent Chaldean was former Deputy Prime Minister Tariq Aziz.

The Syrian Orthodox (37,200) and the Syrian Catholics (55,500, those associated with Rome) have traditionally lived around Mossul, but a majority now lives in Baghdad. The former has three dioceses (Mossul, Basra, Baghdad) and the second two (Mossul and Baghdad).

Other groups include the Armenian Orthodox (25,000), Armenian Catholic (5,000), Latin (5,200), Copt (1,800), Greek Orthodox (800), and Greek Catholic (700).

There are between 5,800 and 13,000 Protestants in Iraq. such as Arab Evangelicals (8,000 members), Presbyterians (3,000 members and 5 churches), and an Armenian Evangelical Church in Baghdad. The Assemblies of God, the Basra Assembly, the Evangelical Alliance of Mission, and the Seventh-day Adventists have churches in Baghdad also.

The Assyrian Church (100,000 members) was the main church of Iraq for centuries, but it has been weakened by persecution and is regarded with great suspicion in Iraq today because of its colonial links to the British. Its leader, the catholicos, lives in Chicago, Illinois.

For more information, see Ray J. Mouawad, "Syria and Iraq: Repression," *The Middle East Quarterly Volume 8:1* (Winter 2001), p. 4.

Then, in 1054 CE, Eastern and Western Christianity split in two over several issues with the most important being structural—who would be the human leader of the Christian church on earth? Eastern Christians put stock in a group of equally authoritative bishops whereas western Christians claimed that one bishop, the Bishop of Rome, had primacy.

Representatives of both east and west excommunicated each other from the faith and for almost 1,000 years did not communicate with one another. From that point on, *Eastern Christianity* went down through history without any major splits and today includes both the Oriental and Eastern Orthodox Christians. However, Western Christianity divided into *Roman* and *Protestant Christianity* between the 1300s and the 1600s CE. Thus, by the 1600s CE, there were, and still are, three major branches of the Christian faith.

## Institutions: Issues

These three divisions of the Christian faith are also the result of beliefs about *Apostolic Succession,* a term employed by Eastern Christians, Roman Catholics, and some Protestants (Anglicans and Lutherans). These Christians believe that there has been an uninterrupted and traceable line of bishops starting with the first apostles. This line is crucial because through this line comes the apostolic authority to ordain valid bishops (and in turn, priests and deacons) and for current bishops (and in turn, priests and deacons) to lead and offici-ate the sacraments with the same authority of the first apostles. This being said, these Christians disagree about which bishops are in true apostolic suc-cession.[13]

Other Protestants do not believe that apostolic succession lies with an unbroken line of bishops stemming from the apostles, even if these groups have bishops. Rather, representing the vast majority of Protestants (including some Anglicans and Lutherans), these believers teach that apostolic succes-sion can be found in those communities of believers where apostolic faith and teaching is maintained.

As a result of different views of apostolic succession, the three branches of the Christian faith have their own views about each other. While all three branches recognize each other as Christians (except perhaps the most ex-treme forms of each), their understanding of each other's Christianities var-ies.

Lacking what is perceived to be true authority, Eastern Christianity labels non-Eastern churches as "communities" of faith, not official churches. Like-wise, Roman Catholics call non-Catholic Christians, in particular Protestants, "separated brethren" only. Given the diverse nature of Protestantism, it is hard to pinpoint the Protestant view of members of the other two branches. However, Protestant positions range from full Christians to unsaved souls.

---

[13] Eastern Churches, Roman Catholics, and Protestants do not recognize the apostol-ic succession of each other's churches.

For the former, non-Protestants are seen as members of another denomination similar to how they view other Protestants. The Protestant view is determined by how much any particular church maintains and teaches true apostolic beliefs and faith.

Today Christians organize in three ways, all having to do with whether the power lies locally, regionally, nationally or internationally. The three are:

- Congregational
- Connectional
- Hierarchical

In *Congregational* government, each local church is independent or "autonomous." All important decisions are made on the local level with all members voting. An excellent example of this form of pure democracy is the totally independent Baptist church. It is not under the authority of any higher-level group, but it is totally on its own.

Previously, one of the best examples of this form of church governance was the Southern Baptist Convention. However, in recent years, local government has surrendered to higher governmental levels when a couple of churches married or ordained practicing homosexuals. These churches were not allowed to follow their own dictates as a local community and remain Southern Baptist. Instead, the Southern Baptist Convention severed ties with them when they refused to renounce their actions.

*Connectional* government is representative rule and functions not unlike the government of the United States. Local congregations (like localities and states) make decisions for themselves. But many major decisions are determined by higher level governing bodies. Presbyterianism has been represented connectional government since John Calvin and John Knox. In Switzerland and Scotland, there were several levels of government running local churches that sent delegates to these different levels of authority. In the United States, local churches send delegates to regional presbyteries, which, in turn, send delegates to national meetings.

In the *Hierarchical* form of church government, bishops hold power. They are either elected by local people or appointed by those higher up in a denomination. Roman Catholicism best represents this form of government with its central leader (i.e., the Pope) and a bureaucracy (the curia) leading the church and appointing local, national, and international leaders.

Christian communities differ on whether or not their pastors, priests, clergy, or ministers should be celibate or may be married. Some, like the Roman Catholic faith, say that their priests and nuns can never marry and must remain chaste. Others say that the choice to marry is up to the minister, which means that most Protestant pastors marry. A third group says that clergy may marry, but this must occur prior to being officially sanctioned or ordained (i.e., Eastern Orthodoxy).

Christian communities differ over the role of women as officially sanctioned clergy and have adopted four approaches:

- Christian churches that have always had ordained women clergy.
- Christian churches that have never ordained women and probably never will.
- Christian churches that used to ordain women and now do not.
- Christian churches that didn't ordain women in the past, but now do.

From the beginning, certain Protestant communities have always ordained women as official clergy with full freedom to officiate the sacraments/ordinances of the church. Examples here include the Cumberland Presbyterians, the Free Will Baptists, the Salvation Army and the Church of the Nazarene. Other churches have done exactly the opposite: Roman Catholicism, Eastern Orthodoxy, the Amish, and the Churches of Christ. Groups like the Southern Baptists and Mennonite Brethren used to have quite a few women pastors, but now do not because they have officially decided against the practice.[14] With congregational government, however, a few Southern Baptist Churches have bucked the system and ordained women pastors anyway. Since the 1960s CE, some, like the mainline Protestant Episcopalian, Methodist, Presbyterian, and Northern or American Baptist, ordain women. In at least one of these groups, the United Methodist Church, more women than men are attending seminary. Groups in the final category tend to get most of the press for the recent inclusion of women. In reality, however, they have been the last to move in a feminist direction.

### SEE WHAT YOU KNOW ABOUT CHRISTIANITY

1. Identify and describe four beliefs.

---

[14] The Southern Baptist church demonstrated its position on women pastors recently when its 100-plus Lifeway Christian bookstores pulled the September, 2008 edition of "Gospel Today" off its shelves because it featured five women pastors on its cover. See Christopher Quinn, "Gospel Today Magazine Pulled from Christian Bookstores' Shelves," *The Atlanta Journal-Constitution* (9/18/2008).

2. Identify and describe three characteristics of lifestyle.

3. Identify and describe four characteristics of ceremonies.

4. Identify and describe three characteristics of institutions.

# CHAPTER II

✠

# EASTERN CHRISTIANITY

## Introduction

The term *Eastern Christianity* refers to those Christian traditions that developed in Greece, the Balkans, Eastern Europe, Asia Minor, India, and the Middle East during the first centuries of the Christian era.[1] Eastern Christianity has five families of churches:

- Oriental Eastern Christians first developed on the easternmost limits of the Byzantine Empire, especially in Egypt and Syria. Oriental Eastern churches can also be found in Armenia, Eritrea, Ethiopia, Egypt, and India.
- The Assyrian Church of the East developed in the Persian Empire.
- Fourteen or fifteen national bodies in communion with the Patriarch of Constantinople are named the Eastern Orthodox.
- Eastern Catholic or Uniat(e) Churches are in communion with the Roman Catholic Church, but practice Eastern traditions (i.e., celibacy is not required of priests).
- A number of small bodies in the East that are offshoots of the major Eastern Churches. Most are related to Russia and are part of the Old Believers Movement.

---

[1] For more information on this topic, see John Philip Jenkins, *The Lost History of Christianity: The Thousand-Year Golden Age of the Church in the Middle East, Africa, and Asia—and How It Died* (New York: Harperone, 2008) and Timothy Ware, *The Orthodox Church: New Edition* (New York: Penguin Books, 1997).

Chapter Two describes what all Eastern Christians have in common. Chapters Three and Four discuss the two major divisions of this branch of the Christian faith:

- Chapter Three: Eastern Oriental Christianity
- Chapter Four: Eastern Orthodox Christianity

### Key Terms

Several key terms help the uninitiated begin to understand the Eastern branch of Christianity. The *Eastern* in the term Eastern Christianity makes a geographic point. Eastern Christianity is composed of churches located in the Eastern Mediterranean basin as well as Eastern Europe or where immigrants of those faiths have traveled outside these areas (i.e., North America, Japan, etc.).

However, Eastern also refers to faithfulness to the beliefs and practices of the early church, which was centered in the eastern Roman Empire in the first centuries CE and in particular, the churches found in the four ancient cities of Alexandria, Antioch, Jerusalem, and Constantinople. Eastern also refers to the locations of seven churchwide or ecumenical councils held by the Christian church in the first 1,000 years of Christian history. Two were in Nicea, three in Constantinople, one at Ephesus and one at Chalcedon. Eastern Christians handle these councils in a variety of ways.[2]

*Mystery* is an important component of the faith. For Eastern Christians, there is a fundamental mystery to faith questions, such as who is God, how does salvation occur, does transubstantiation occur during the Eucharist or what does the intense smell of incense symbolize? To try to fully explain such things is an impossible and unnecessary task. Christians should live in the mystery.

Another key word is the number *Three*, which is said to symbolize the key term "Trinity." Eastern Christians do many things in threes to emphasize this term. For examples, churches have three sections, marriage has three purposes and individuals are immersed three times in baptismal waters. In some Eastern groups, a person has up to three times to establish a valid marriage.

*Icon* is a significant term for Eastern Christianity. Icons are often fuzzy two-dimensional representations of Jesus, Mary, and other saints. The devout

---

[2] The Seven Ecumenical Councils are: Nicea I (325 CE), Constantinople I (381 CE), Ephesus (431 CE), Chalcedon (451 CE), Constantinople II (553 CE), Constantinople III (681 CE), and Nicea II (787 CE).

Oriental Easterners accept only three Ecumenical Councils (Nicea—325, Constantinople—381, and Ephesus—431) and they explicitly reject the declarations of Chalcedon (451). The Assyrian Church of the East accepts only Nicea (325) and the First Council of Constantinople (381). The Eastern Orthodox accept all seven Ecumenical Councils.

carry them in processions, light candles in their presence, bow before them, and even kiss them. Eastern Christians do not worship these representations, but venerate them (i.e., honor or show respect). By 843 CE, the church had decided that icons were not idols, but instead pointed the devout toward God. Thus, they could be used in worship in a similar fashion to other material symbols, such as the cross and the Bible.[3] As a result, the typical Eastern church is filled with icons and candles present before them.

*The Dimension of a Religious Object* is also an important idea in Eastern Christianity. As opposed to western churches, which have two or three-dimensional objects (height, width, and depth), Eastern churches generally have two dimensional objects (height and width, not depth).

This has occurred for many reasons. First, Eastern churches want the worship of God to be focused on God himself not on statues of important church leaders or biblical characters. Also, Eastern churches stress mystery and paintings are more mysterious than free-standing statues. Third, early Christians believed that Christian art needed to be very different than pagan art. They thought that demons or "daimones" lived in pagan three-dimensional sculptures. So, they made two-dimensional objects. Finally, in order to avoid the commandment not to make "graven images," Eastern paintings may never be more than three-quarter bas relief.

Another key term is *Ethnic.* Of the three major branches of Christendom, Eastern Christianity is the most ethnically oriented. To be a member of one of these churches, a person almost has to be from one of the ethnic groups represented, such as Russian, Bulgarian, Greek, or Romanian.

The concept *orthodox* with a small "o" is also an important concept in Eastern Christianity. This term means "correct" or "right." When this branch of Christianity speaks of being correct or right it means correct or right in terms of having the most correct worship, beliefs, and organization because it is the closest to the original form of the earliest church.[4] Being correct or right also refers to the living Eastern Christians being the heirs, guardians, and transmitters of a great inheritance to the next generation.

Two final key words are *Orthodox* and *Oriental* both spelled with a capital "O." From the outset of the Christian faith, believers struggled to understand how Jesus could be fully God and fully human at the same time. Some argued that Jesus was not divine (Arianism), that his humanity was so separated from his divinity that he was fully two persons instead of one (Nestorianism), or that Jesus had no human nature or will (Monophysitism, Monthelitism). The

---

[3] For more details on the controversy concerning icons, see J. D. Douglas, General Editor, *The International Dictionary of the Christian Church*, 2nd ed. (Grand Rapids: Zondervan Publishing House, 1978), p. 498.
[4] See appendix for a typical view of church history from the Eastern perspective (at least the Orthodox part of the Eastern community).

terms Orthodox and Oriental, both spelled with a capital "O," highlight differences of interpretation in this important matter by eastern groups.[5]

The Western Church and those which accept the leadership of the Patriarch of Constantinople adopted the resolution of the *Council of Chalcedon* in 451 CE This meeting declared that Christ had two natures "unconfusedly, unchangeably, indivisibly, inseparably; the differences between the natures is in no way removed because of their union, but rather the peculiar property of each is preserved, and both combine in one." In other words, Christ had two unique, separate, eternal, indissoluble natures. Each, the divine and human, maintain their differences and yet both combine into one. These churches include the Roman Catholic Church, Protestant churches, and the Churches of Constantinople, Antioch, Alexandria, Jerusalem, Cyprus, Russia, Hungary, Greece, Sinai, Bulgaria, Serbia, Austria, Rumania, Bosnia, Herzegovina, and Japan. Of these churches, the eastern ones use the term Orthodox with a capital "O."

For the others, the Oriental churches, any statement that stated that Jesus had two separate natures, even if they were combined, diminished Jesus' stature as a human and divine being. Believing that the Lord's divinity and humanity are each absolute, Oriental Christians maintain that they are unified in one nature, "the Nature of the Incarnate Word." The human and divine are united in one "without mingling, without confusion, and without alteration." Further, the human and divine "did not separate for a moment or the twinkling of an eye."[6]

### Beliefs

Eastern Christians believe that the final authority for what beliefs to hold and what practices to carry out is located in the Bible and the tradition of the church until Christendom split either in the 500s CE (for the Oriental Christians) or in 1054 CE (for the Orthodox Christians). Since these times, the truth of Christianity has not been as clearly seen. Eastern Christians use the illustration comparing the refraction of rays of light rather than unrefracted, direct rays of light to argue for their understanding of final authority.

---

[5] A recent interview with an Oriental priest emphasized the significance of this theological debate. Slamming his fist on his office desk, the priest stated quite emphatically, "Not for one twinkling of eye has the divine and human in Jesus been separated. That would make Jesus less than who is really is." So much for ancient church debates disappearing over time!

[6] The last two quotes are taken directly from an English translation of the Coptic Liturgy just before a believer takes the bread and wine. *Oriental Orthodox Sometimes Called Non-Chalcedonian Eastern Christians*, Orchid Land Publications (2001), pp. 1-2.

Because contemporary eastern Bibles are based on the Septuagint, they contain the Apocrypha.[7] Some eastern communities add more books. For example, the Oriental Ethiopian Orthodox Church has 81 books instead of the accepted 66 (see Chapter Three).

Eastern Christians venerate the biblical text by prostrating themselves before it, kissing it, putting it in a place of honor on the altar, carrying it in procession, standing when it is read, and constantly reading it.

For Eastern Christians, tradition is found in many documents, including patriarchal pronouncements, chants, prayers, and creeds. Part of tradition consists of documents from the ecumenical councils of the early church with the most important being those from the Council of Nicea in 325 CE.

Also, Eastern Christians cite the *Church Fathers* extensively. These were writers and thinkers from the first several centuries of Christian history who helped shape the movement and are recognized by all Christians. Although the exact names and number of these Church Fathers is unclear, three are of particular significance for Orthodoxy: Basil the Great, Gregory of Nazianzus, and John Chrysostom (the so-called "Three Hierarchs").

Salvation involves several aspects. First, Jesus did not die to deal with God's requirements for divine justice, the judicial view that Roman Catholics and Protestants teach. Instead, Jesus died to make humans more like God, not gods themselves. This lifetime process is called *Deification*. An image popular among Eastern Christians is a foggy mirror. The image of God in each person is fogged up due to sin and it is un-fogged in the process of deification. This un-fogging involves two things taken together: faith in Christ's sacrifice for sins and godly works, such as receiving God's grace in the sacraments and loving one's neighbors.

Eastern Christians believe in two, not three immediate destinations—heaven and hell, not purgatory, heaven and hell.

Saints are important to Eastern Christians. Eastern Christians venerate saints, seek to copy their pious lives, and name their children, special holidays, and churches after them. Many Eastern Christians pray to the saints. They do not merely honor them for their obedience to God, like most Protestants. Mary, the mother of Jesus, is honored as the *Theotokos* or "God-Bearer."

---

[7] For a recent example, see *The Orthodox Study Bible: Ancient Christianity Speaks to Today's World* (Nashville: Thomas Nelson, 2008).

### Eastern Ways of Life [8]

Eastern lifestyles are influenced more often by ethnicity than the religion itself.

That being said, certain approaches to ethics and actual ways of life mark almost all Eastern Christians. Eastern Christians think about the following concerns when articulating ethical concerns.

The first question has to do with sources: which sources should be used to create an ethical system and how should those sources be used? The Eastern faith believes that sources created before the East-West split in the 500s CE or in 1054 CE reflect the truest teachings of Christ. Everything afterward is less authoritative and hence of secondary value. This means, for example, that Orthodoxy accepts the Bible and church tradition until 1054 CE as equally valid, authoritative sources. This includes the Bible, the writings of early Church Fathers, the teachings of the Seven Ecumenical Councils, the monastic tradition of the church, canon law, the liturgies, and sacraments. Any church tradition or human wisdom (i.e., the social sciences such as psychology, sociology, and medical developments) arising later is helpful, but not central.

This Eastern methodology presents particular issues when dealing with ethical questions that have arisen since 1054 CE, such as cloning or nuclear weapons. With these issues, the Orthodox believer looks for principles in the pre-1054 CE documents that can apply to the modern situation. For example, according to the Orthodox tradition the Bible and tradition teach that each individual is a unique creation of God. Therefore human cloning in any form is unacceptable.

Another question is: because the Trinity is so important to Eastern Christianity, "What is its relationship to ethics?" For the Eastern Christian, the Trinity is seen as a community of persons who have a good relationship with each other. This separate, yet unified threesome serves as a model for all humans and, in fact, all creation. None is jealous of the other; none is secondary to the other. Each individual is distinct and yet connected. Just as the Trinity gets along, so should humans.

Given the importance of the Trinity, the question is asked: "What is the relationship of each person in the Trinity to ethics?" To the Eastern believer, God the Father creates the necessity, will, and potential for ethical possibili-

---

[8] For the material found in this section, I am grateful for the work of one of the leading Orthodox ethicists, Stanley S. Harakas. His most significant writings include: *Wholeness of Faith and Life* (Brookline, Mass.: Holy Cross Orthodox Press, 1999); *Living the Faith: The Praxis of Eastern Orthodox Ethics* (Minneapolis, MN: Light and Life Pub., 1992); *Health and Medicine in the Eastern Orthodox Tradition : Faith, Liturgy, and Wholeness* (New York: Crossroad, 1990); *Let Mercy Abound : Social Concern in the Greek Orthodox Church* (Brookline, Mass.: Holy Cross Orthodox Press, 1983); *Toward Transfigured Life: The Theoria of Eastern Orthodox Ethics* (Minneapolis: Light and Life Pub. , 1983); and *Contemporary Moral Issues Facing the Orthodox Christian* (Minneapolis: Light and Life Pub., 1982).

ties. Jesus makes this possible through his teaching, control over nature, his submission to demonic forces with his death on the cross, and his victory over all by his resurrection. In Jesus, God saves humanity as a whole, providing forgiveness and the restoration of the divine-likeness in all creation. Jesus' salvation is both individual and corporate. The third person of the Trinity, the Holy Spirit provides power to be moral.

The Eastern Christian asks, "In what ways are humans connected to God and how can humans become ethical?" Humans are made in God's image and share in the divine attributes of intelligence, self-determination, moral perceptivity, creativity, and the capacity for human relationships. Humans have been given the ability or potential to become like God, not to be God themselves. However, sin or the prideful rebellion of humans against God, has kept them from God-like status and has clouded their soul. The image of God is not totally lost, rather much of it covered by sin. The Orthodox compares this clouding to the fog that accumulates on a mirror in a bathroom when a shower is run. The mirror is still a mirror and can still reflect the image of the person looking at it, but it is clouded over by fog just as the soul can still reflect God's image, but it is clouded by sin. Human beings can become more moral as they wipe off the fog on the mirror of their soul and more closely resemble God's image.

Part of the process of deification involves human ability to act morally, using the conscience. The Eastern Christian believes that each person's innate ability establishes ethical categories and makes moral judgments. Sometimes this is called "moral drive" or "ethical sense." Part of this moral obligation is the conscience, which has the potential to resemble God's sense of moral obligation. However, without salvation, the human conscience can be deformed and/or underdeveloped.

The Eastern Christian asks, "Why are some non-Christians moral and how can Christians and non-Christians live morally in the world?" The Eastern church teaches that a natural moral law exists. All humanity and all creation have a fundamental set of established patterns or basic norms of existence. These are universally defined in all societies, cultures, and groups. This law is found in all religions and in particular in Judaism in the Ten Commandments. An example would be, "You shall not kill," a principle common to all societies.

Another question has to do with the role of the church in the creation of ethics. Simply put, its task is to deify human beings and all creation. The church's job is to assist the individual to discover the motives and behavior that are appropriate for a person seeking deification. The church should never be legalistic when helping individuals or society "unfog their mirrors." Eastern Christianity's leadership style also contributes to how the church should foster ethical individuals or societies. It does not have one authoritative leader. Instead, a college of bishops leads the Eastern faith. They meet together to discuss particular issues and then make pronouncements. These pronouncements are carried out somewhat autocratically in each branch of the faith.

A final question has to do with the role of Christians and the church in society: "Should the church be involved in politics and should it take positions on social issues, such as feminism or gay rights?"

For the most part, Eastern Christians are actively involved in society and culture. However, exceptions include those living in monastic communities and also those times and places where the civil rights of Eastern churches have been or are being curtailed, such as in some Muslim countries.

The Eastern church has had a long history of close church-state relationships. Since the beginning it has been closely linked with many governments under the form of *Caesaropapism*, where the church and state are virtually one institution, each as separate departments with distinct functions. This was most typified in Czarist Russia. Eastern Christianity is just now learning to exist in cultures that have separation of church and state amidst a plurality of equally competing religions.

Eastern Christianity teaches that social justice issues are important and should be part of individual and church life. This arises from two ideas. First, through his agapé love as demonstrated in the incarnation of Jesus, God took the time and energy to send his son to save the world. This action encourages believers to fight to make society a better place. Another source to carry out social justice is derived from the idea that saved humanity should help unsaved humanity and suffering society achieve the potential of God-likeness or deification. When working to improve society, Eastern Christianity rarely calls for radical social transformation. Instead, it is individualistic. Changed or deified humans should individually change society.

### Ceremonies

Eastern Christianity is a liturgical community of faith. It claims to follow the most ancient patterns of worship. There is a heavy use of incense and chanting with fancy-robbed clergy, occurring in very ornate churches, generally shaped in the form of a cross. The continual repetition of *The Jesus Prayer* resounds, "Lord Jesus Christ, Son of God, have mercy on me."

Eastern Christians use the *Julian* rather than Gregorian calendar. Because of this, their dates for the celebration of Easter and Christmas often fall a week or two later than Western Christians.

In Orthodoxy, the *Divine Liturgy* is the main worship service. It takes up to three hours and the devout normally stand for the entire time. Some, like American churches, have added the use of pews and chairs. The devout are not required to attend for all three hours.

There are three parts to the Divine Liturgy. Part one, "the Office of Preparation," involves preparing the communion elements by a priest and deacon without a congregation in a special chapel, the Chapel of Prothesis. The second part, "the Synaxis," contains the Little Entrance, where the Gospels are taken around the church just prior to reading them. Following are scripture readings, the sermon, and last, intercessory prayers.

In the last and third part of the Divine Liturgy, there is the "Grand Entrance" (when the priest takes the elements from the Prothesis to the altar), the Kiss of Peace, and a communal reciting of the Nicene Creed. Then, the priest takes the bread and wine behind the iconostasis or altar curtain and consecrates the elements. It is during this time that transubstantiation occurs, although Orthodoxy refrains from making this a dogma as Rome has.[9]

The priest then places the bread in the chalice of wine. The bread-filled chalice is brought out and carried through the people. All who can, from infant to old age, take some of the bread soaked wine from the priest with one spoon. The communion is closed, meaning only Eastern Christians can participate. However, non-Orthodox may be offered *Antidoron* or blessed bread as a sign of fellowship. Any part of the sacrament that is left over is placed or reserved in a tabernacle for later use with the sick who could not attend church.

There are seven sacraments in Eastern Christianity. These *Holy Mysteries* have sacramental significance; that is, in each mystery the devout get a zap of God's grace.

Baptism is mostly for infants. It is normally done at the entrance of the church's sanctuary to symbolize the newly baptized status at the door of the church prior to baptism. The infant is immersed three times to symbolize the Trinity and then in the second mystery, Chrismation, the infant is immediately anointed with oil, which symbolizes the Holy Spirit.

The third mystery is the Eucharist. Another mystery is that of penance, in which the believer's sins are forgiven by God through a priest. Here, the emphasis is on helping the individual move along in the deification process, to unfog the penitent's mirror.

The ordination of men to the priesthood is the fifth sacrament. This gives an individual the grace to perform the sacraments and to be pastoral leaders. Priests may marry if they are as such prior to priestly ordination. If a priest wants to be a bishop, he must remain unmarried. There are monks and nuns who live separate from their local cultures and focus more on scholarship and spirituality. This distinguishes them from their western counterparts who focus more on social service.

Marriage is another mystery. Heterosexual marriage is the only sexual outlet permitted in Eastern Christianity. Marriage is highly esteemed and believers may marry baptized non-Eastern Christians, but they may not marry non-Christians. In Orthodoxy, if they do, they cannot receive the sacraments or serve as godparents for Orthodox children. In some Orthodox communities, members have up to three times to establish a valid marriage (i.e., the

---

[9] For the definition of transubstantiation, see the Roman Catholic chapter.

"three strikes and you're out rule"). Second and third marriages, after divorces, are not celebrated as festively as first ones.

A unique part of the marriage ceremony involves the crowning of the bride and groom. This symbolizes that the new couple participates in the kingship of Christ and that they are martyrs in the biblical sense, meaning witnesses to Christ as a couple.

In the last and seventh mystery, the sick and dying are anointed. They receive the zap of grace to help them be healed or to prepare them for death.

## Institutions

Eastern Christians have self-headed or *Autocephalous* churches. Each church is therefore autonomous and each church chief leader has equal authority with others in authority. These churches can be found in geographic areas (Armenia, Ethiopia, Egypt, Iran), in ancient cities of the East (Jerusalem, Antioch, Alexandria, Constantinople), among national churches such as the Greek, Romanian, Russian, and Croatian Orthodox communities and in recent years, throughout the world, including Middle Tennessee.

Each geographic, city, and national church is headed by a patriarch (the title may vary) and is hierarchical. Oriental churches are much more independent of each other than their Orthodox counterparts, although their leaders have started consultations. The Ethiopians and the Egyptians have a special relationship given that the latter helped establish and lead the Ethiopian church until the 20th century CE.

For those churches linked to the *Patriarch of Constantinople*, the Patriarch of Constantinople has "primacy among equals." He is first in the potluck line and has the fanciest seat in the house. Before 1054 CE, there were five ancient Christian cities all equals. Now there are four because one city, Rome, has asserted its primacy over the others. Orthodoxy (and Oriental Christians) does not accept the authority of the Bishop of Rome or the Pope. Leaders are waiting until the Roman Church realizes that its claim to having the one leader of the church on earth is false and then they will ask the Roman Church to rejoin their community.

Orthodoxy has also worked hard to reestablish relationships with the Oriental churches and has met with some success.[10]

---

[10] For examples of this dialogue, see Damaskinos Papandreou, "Oriental Orthodox-Roman Catholic Dialogue: Historical Introduction," *Growth in Agreement II: Reports and Agreed Statements of Ecumenical Conversations on a World Level 1982 – 1998*, ed. by Jeffrey Gros, Harding Meyer, William G. Rusch, *Faith and Order Paper* No. 187 (Grand Rapids, MI: William B. Eerdmans Publishing Company, 2000), p. 688; Theodore Pulcini, "Recent Strides Towards Reunion of the Eastern and Oriental Churches: Healing the Chalcedonian Breach," *Journal of Ecumenical Studies* 30:1 (Winter 1993), pp. 37-8; and "Fourth Unofficial Consultation Between Oriental Orthodox and Eastern Orthodox Theologians, Addis Ababa, January 22-23, 1971," *Greek Orthodox Theological Review* 16: 1-2 (1971), p. 213.

## SEE WHAT YOU KNOW ABOUT EASTERN CHRISTIANITY

1. Identify and describe four beliefs.

2. Identify and describe three characteristics of lifestyle.

3. Identify and describe four characteristics of ceremonies.

4. Identify and describe three characteristics of institutions.

# CHAPTER III
✠
# EASTERN ORIENTAL CHRISTIANITY

In the fifth and sixth centuries CE, Oriental churches split off from the other eastern Christian communities thanks to divisions of culture, geography, and theology (i.e., the relationship of the human and divine in Jesus Christ). Today, these Christians fall into two groups:

- The Church of the East with approximately 550,000 members (mainly today in Iraq and Iran), sometimes called the Assyrian, Nestorian, Chaldean, or East Syrian Churches.

- The non-Chalcedonian churches with approximately 27 million members (frequently wrongly called Monophysite): the Syrian Church of Antioch (Jacobite Church), the Syrian Church in India, the Coptic Church in Egypt, the Armenian Church, the Ethiopian Church, and the Eritrean Churches.[1]

---

[1] The Church of the East located mainly in Iraq and Iran, has a leader called the Catholicos-Patriarch, who lives in Chicago. The church has four archdioceses throughout the world and many monasteries. The Syrian language is used, but it is written in another alphabet. This church believes that the Aramaic text of the Bible (Peschitta) is the most reliable and calls Mary the Mother of Christ (christotokos) instead of Mother of God (theotokos).

The Armenian Apostolic Church traditionally says that St. Thaddeus and St. Bartholomew established the church in Armenia. Armenia claims to be the first nation to accept Christianity (301) through the earlier ministry of St. Gregory the Illuminator. Armenian Christians have suffered terrible persecutions over the centuries and many have fled. Armenian nationalism and religion are fused. Their Catholicos of All Armenians lives in Etchmiadzin, Armenia and there are three other centers (Cilicia, Jerusalem, and Constantinople).

Two examples of Oriental churches that will be explored here are the Christian Coptic Church of Egypt, and the Ethiopian Orthodox Tewahedo Bete Christian.

## The Christian Coptic Orthodox Church of Egypt

The word *Copt* comes from the Greek word "Aigyptos," which in turn, was derived from "Hikaptah," one of the names for Memphis, the first capital of ancient Egypt. In modern use, the term is used for Egyptian Christians as well as the last stage of the ancient Egyptian language script and the art and architecture that arose thanks to early Egyptian Christianity.

### History and Beliefs

According to tradition, the founder of the Coptic Church is the biblical character *Mark*, who brought the faith to Egypt just a few years after Christ's resurrection during the reign of the Roman Emperor Nero (37-68 CE).

Members of the Coptic Church point out that there are several biblical citations referring to Egypt. The nation is the subject of many biblical prophecies, such as Isaiah 19:19, "In that day there will be an altar to the Lord in the midst of the land of Egypt, and a pillar to the Lord at its border." Also, Egypt was the only nation outside of Israel that Jesus visited during his human life

---

The Syriac Orthodox Church (also called the Syrian Orthodox Church of Antioch) traces its history back to 37 CE and St. Peter. It has been mistakenly called Jacobite. Because of terrible persecutions, its see has had to move several times, but now it is in Damascus. In 1665 CE, the church linked up with the St. Thomas Christians of India and gave them the West Syrian liturgy. The Indian branch of this church is called the Malankara Syriac Orthodox Church (also called by a variety of names, such as the Jacobite Syrian Church, Malankara Jacobite Syrian Orthodox Church). It is located in Kerala, India.

The Malankara (Indian) Orthodox Church of India (also called by a variety of names, such as the Malankara Orthodox Syrian Church or the Syrian Church in India) believes that it was founded by St. Thomas in 52 CE in Kerala, India. It took on a Syrian form after 1665 CE, but in 1912 CE finally declared itself independent of Syria. The Malankara Church has a theological college, a mission training center and many educational and charitable institutions. Its members tend to have higher socioeconomic status than other Indians. Its catholicos resides in Kottayam, Kerala. The church has 20 bishops and more than 1,000 local churches.

The Eritrean Orthodox Church was established in 1993 CE when Eritrea declared its independence from Ethiopia. Until then, it was the largest diocese of the Church of Ethiopia. The Eritrean Church has 1.7 million members, 1,500 churches, 22 monasteries and 15,000 priests.

Some Eastern Oriental Churches are autonomous and in communion with the Roman Catholic Church: The Byzantine (Melkite, Ruthenan, Bulgarian, Romanian, and Italo-Greco Christians), Chaldean, Alexandrian, Abyssinian, Syrian, Armenian, and Marionite Catholics as well as the Uniats of Malabar and the Ukraine.

(Matthew 2:15). Yet, Egyptian Christians are the first to say that biblical references to Egypt are a double-edged sword. Copts are quick to remind the curious that the Egyptians were the "bad guys" in the Moses story.

For the four centuries that followed the Arab/Islamic conquest of Egypt, the Coptic Church prospered and Egypt remained basically Christian. This was due to Muhammad who told his followers to treat Copts well because the prophet had an Egyptian wife. But from the beginning, *Islam* has placed great limits on religious freedom (i.e., practice privately, do no evangelize, pay taxes to the Islamic state, and send Christian children to Islamic schools) and slowly, but surely, Islamic culture and religion (which in the Islamic mind are one) became the dominant one in numbers and influence.

Egyptian Christian contributions to Christendom are numerous. From its beginning it has played a central role in the development of Christian beliefs and practices, especially when protecting the faith from *Gnostics*.[2] The Egyptian church produced thousands of texts and biblical and theological studies that are used by contemporary archaeologists. Hundreds of scribes copied manuscripts into Coptic and these are found today in libraries throughout the world. Early Christian leaders from Egypt played a significant role in Christian development, like Athanasius, Pope of Alexandria from 327-373 CE *Monasticism* was born in Egypt and spread from there both East and West. The world's first Christian monk was St. Anthony, a Copt from Upper Egypt. Copts have moved in to the pinnacle of world power and influence in recent years. Dr. Boutros Boutros-Ghali was the sixth General-Secretary of the United Nations (1992-1997 CE) and Dr. Magdi Habib Yacoub was one of the world's most renowned heart surgeons.

## Coptic Ways of Life

Members of the Coptic Church are by-and-large Egyptian and therefore follow the ways of living common to that culture.

The Church does not have (and actually refuses to canonize) official positions on controversial issues, such as abortion. While the church's teachings are clear (abortion interferes with God's will and is wrong), the Coptic

---

[2] This term is used for a variety of religious movements both inside and outside early Christianity which taught that creation was evil and God was good. Creation contained sparks of divinity, but these were trapped in creation, especially in certain humans. God sent a redeemer, a Christ of Spirit only, who by giving out secret knowledge or "gnosis," liberated these sparks of divinity. Then humans achieved salvation. For many Gnostics, Christ did not die on the cross because God would not have put himself in evil flesh. Instead, Christ's role was as initiator into truth and then liberation. Because salvation did not depend on one's behavior, but instead upon secret knowledge, Gnostics could be either extremely loose sexually or celibate (i.e., marriage and sex were part of creation and inherently evil).

faith still argues that such matters are best taken care of on a case-by-case basis through a "Father of Confession," rather than by church rule.[3]

### Coptic Ceremonies

The main Coptic service is held on Sunday and can last from three to six hours. It has five parts:

- The Preparation Prayer: Lasting thirty minutes, altar boys circle the altar chanting in Coptic with incense.

- The Offering: Lasting twenty to thirty minutes, a prayer is said over the holy bread.

- The Preaching Mass: At this time, priests read sections of the Old and New Testaments and give a sermon.

- The Reconciliation Prayer: Lasting ten minutes, this is when the Priest offers the congregation Christ's forgiveness and asks the people to forgive each other.

- The Believer's Mass: The congregation has communion.

Men and women sit on opposite sides of the church during most services and they go to different sides of the altar to take communion. Women wear head coverings.

Copts observe seven sacraments: Baptism, Chrismation (Confirmation), Eucharist, Confession (Penance), Orders, Matrimony, and Unction of the Sick.

- Baptism: Performed normally on infants, who are immersed three times in a font at the entrance to the church.

- Confirmation: Performed immediately after baptism by a priest who places oil on the head of the newly baptized.

---

[3] Eastern Christians tend to choose individuals to be spiritual guides. They can serve as "Spiritual Fathers" or "Spiritual Mothers." Individuals turn to these guides for confession, prayer, and advice.

- Eucharist:

The highlight of each liturgy with bread mushed into one chalice of wine. Believers go to the front and take the two elements with one spoon. Closed communion is practiced.

- Confession:

Regular confession with a personal priest is carried out. The family usually chooses this personal priest (the Father of Confession). A person must confess before taking the Eucharist.

- Orders:

A bishop lays hands on the would-be deacon, priest, or bishop so that the Holy Spirit will grant him one of the ranks of clergy with the authority to carry out the sacraments of the church.

- Matrimony

Marriage for life, but divorce is allowed for adultery or other extreme situations. This must be reviewed by a Council of Bishops. Either the husband or wife can ask for a divorce. The church does not recognize civil divorce. Polygamy or other sexual practices are not permitted even if the state allows.

- Unction of the Sick

Wearing a priestly robe (epitrachelion), the priest administers confession prior to the prayer for the sick. Facing East, the priest then offers seven short prayers, recites a blessing and the Lord's Prayer. After, he anoints the sick with oil on their forehead, chest, and hands and makes the sign of the Cross. It is recommended that the person prayed for takes the Eucharist as soon as possible. Unction for the Sick is meant to heal the soul first, which in turn may heal the body.

The Coptic Church has three main liturgies: The Liturgy of St. Basil, the Bishop of Caesarea; the Liturgy of Saint Gregory of Nazianzus, the Bishop of Constantinople; and the Liturgy of St. Cyril, the 24th Pope of the Coptic Church. The most popular is the first, but all three are in regular use with added sections (intercessions). The *Coptic Language* is the liturgical language of the church.

The Coptic Church does not worship saints, but it venerates them and asks for their aid. Asking the saints for assistance is a central part of any Coptic liturgy. Coptic churches are named after a patron saint.

The most popular saint is Virgin Saint Mary. She is labeled the theotokos or the "God-bearer." According to Coptic tradition, Mary has appeared to the faithful. Her repeated appearances atop the dome of St. Mary's Church in the Cairo suburb of Zeitoun for three years beginning in 1968 CE were seen by thousands of Muslim and Christian believers.[4]

The religious calendar of the Coptic Church is based on the calendar system used by the ancient pharaohs of Egypt (i.e., for the division of the year into three major periods and for dating the years).

Martyr's Days also fill the Coptic calendar and the calendar itself is called the "Calendar of the Martyrs." Its starting date is November, 284 CE, when Diocletian was made Roman Emperor. Due to the large number of Christians murdered, Diocletian's reign is known as "the Era of the Martyrs."

However, Copts claim that persecution began on May 8, 68 CE On this date, Roman soldiers forced their Patron Saint Mark (the biblical character) through the streets and then killed him. Almost every ruler of Egypt has persecuted the church. Their clergy has been tortured and scattered, even by fellow Christians (for not agreeing to the Council of Chalcedon). For Copts, the fact the church has survived is proof of the validity of its faith.

The church year is composed of moveable and immovable feast and fast days.[5] There are seven major and seven minor feasts. The seven major feasts include: Annunciation, Christmas, Theophany (Epiphany in western churches), Palm Sunday, Easter, Ascension, and Pentecost. Christmas is celebrated on January 7. Easter is usually on the second Sunday after the first full moon in the Spring and may be celebrated with more enthusiasm than Christmas.

Days or periods of fasting fill the Coptic calendar (210 of 365 days are fast days). On many fast days, no animal products are allowed (meat, poultry, fish, milk, eggs, butter, etc.). Also, no food or drink can be ingested between sunrise and sunset. Priests can lessen these requirements for lay people as

---

[4] http://www.unexplainedstuff.com/Religious-Phenomena/Mother-Mary-Appears-in-Egypt.html

[5] Movable celebrations are those annual celebrations that occur on different dates each year depending on things such as the timing of the equinox. Immovable holidays are celebrated on the same date each year, regardless of what day of the week they occur.

needed. Fasting seasons include the Fast of the Nativity for 45 days (Christmas), the Fast of the Apostles, the Fast of the Virgin Mary, the Fast of Nineveh and Lent, known as "the Great Fast." This lasts for 55 days.

Copts pray for the reunion of all Christians daily in their churches. Prayer is also offered for Egypt and its river (the Nile), crops, president, army, government and its people.

## Coptic Institutions

Late in the 20th century, there are approximately 9 million Copts out of a population of 57 million Egyptians. There are thousands of local churches throughout Egypt. In addition, 1.2 million live throughout the world.[6]

The *Pope of Alexandria* is the head of the church. He is not seen as infallible. Bishops oversee priests ordained in their dioceses. Both the pope and the bishops must also be monks and are celibate. Today over 60 Coptic bishops govern dioceses inside Egypt as well as outside, such as in Jerusalem, Sudan, Western Africa, Europe, Great Britain, and the United States. Priests have direct responsibility for local congregations. They can be married and must have attended a Catechetical School prior to ordination.

The pope and the bishops meet regularly in the *Coptic Orthodox Holy Synod* to oversee the church. Two other non-clerical bodies help govern the church. The *Coptic Lay Council* is popularly elected. Beginning in 1883 CE, it has acted as an intermediary between the Church and the government. The second is a joint clerical-lay committee to direct the management of the church's endowments according to Egyptian law. This was begun in 1928 CE.

## The Ethiopian Orthodox Tewahido Church: History

Ethiopia has a lengthy Christian tradition beginning with references to the nation and her people in the Bible, where it is mentioned 38 times. For example, Genesis 2:11-13 calls it the "Land of Cush." According to the Bible, one of the earliest converts to Christianity was an Ethiopian eunuch in Queen Candice's service who was converted and then baptized in the desert by Philip (Acts 8:26-40).

The link between Judaism and Ethiopian Christianity and culture is important. The *Kebre Negest* (*The Glory of the Kings*) highlights some of these connections by asserting:

- Ethiopian kings are descendants from Solomon via Sheba.
- The original Ark of the Covenant was brought from Jerusalem to Ethiopia (by either Levites or by having been stolen by Menelik 1, the son of Solomon and Sheba).

---

[6] http://www.touregypt.net/featurestories/copticchristians.htm

- The God of Israel transferred his actual presence to Ethiopia from Jerusalem.

As a result, Ethiopians believe that the original Ark is housed in the *Chapel of the Tablet at the Church of Our Lady Mary of Zion in Axum*, the holiest shrine in the nation.[7] A monk called the "Keeper of the Ark" guards the ark.[8]

Axum is where Menelik I established his Solomonic dynasty that lasted until the 1970s CE.[9] Many contend that the ark protects them from harm both as individuals and as a nation. They would prove this by showing that Ethiopia was the only African nation that did not fall under the control of a European nation during the 19th century CE.

History records that two brothers, *Frumentius* and *Edesius* of Tyre (Phoenicia), were taken as prisoners to Abyssinia (Ethiopia) in the 4th century CE, where they eventually gained the favor of the Emperor Ezana. They were set free and began to evangelize. About 340 CE, Bishop Athanasius of Alexandria made Frumentius the first bishop of Ethiopia. At the close of the 5th century, 9 monks came from Syria and the Ethiopian Church formally adopted the non-Chalcedonian position. The church was cut off from other Christians both East and West, except for the Coptic Church. Rising Islamic influence, connections with the Coptic Church, and geographic isolation were significant factors in the church's development.

---

[7] In ancient times, the Hebrew people believed that the Ark of the Covenant contained the presence of God. It was a box, which contained tablets of the Law, and it had angels resting on either side of the top. Between them was the lid, which was called the mercy seat. The ark was placed first in the roving tabernacle and then with few exceptions was housed in the main Jerusalem Temple.

Not only is the current whereabouts of the ark the subject of Ethiopian belief, but it is also the subject of academic theory and even movies. Leen Ritmeyer, an archaeologist, argues that the Ark of the Covenant is buried deep within the Temple Mound (see Leen Ritmeyer, "The Ark of the Covenant: Where it Stood in Solomon's Temple" *Biblical Archaeology Review* 22:1 [1996], pp. 46-55, 70-73). For movie buffs, the 1981 blockbuster *Raiders of the Lost Ark* has its own rendition of the history of the ark.

[8] The "Keeper of the Ark" prays before the ark, day and night, with burning incense. No one else can see the ark besides this person. The "Keeper of the Ark" is chosen by Axum's senior priests and the present guardian. According to one Smithsonian story, "In the mid-twentieth century a chosen guardian had run away, terrified, and had to be hauled back to Aksum." For more information, see http://www.smithsonianmag.com/people-places/ark-covenant-200712.html?c=y&page=4

[9] Menelik's dynasty officially lasted until 1974 with the disestablishment of the monarchy. It was claimed that Haille Sellasse I (1892-1975 CE) also called the Conquering Lion of Judah, was the 225th direct descendent of Solomon (and Sheba). His son, Amha Sellasse I (1916-1997 CE), was the 226th descendant and his grandson and current claimant to the throne, Zera Yacob Amha Sellasse (1953- CE) asserts that he is the 227th claimant. He lives in Ethiopia, but he is not the nation's ruler.

## Beliefs

Ethiopian Christians believe that the Bible is the inspired Word of God. It contains *81 books*. These include 46 Old Testament and 35 New Testament books. The Ethiopian Bible contains the same Apocryphal books as some other Christians, but they may add some extras depending on how the canon is understood.[10] Other books include: eight books of church order (decisions by church councils called Synodos) and a large collection of books, including the *Kebre Negest (Glory of Kings)*, the *Book of Henoch (Kufale* or *Little Genesis)*, the *Book of the Mysteries of Heaven and Earth*, the *Combat of Adam and Eve* and the *Ascension of Isaiah*.

Along with the first Ethiopian Bible (from the 5th century CE), the most important religious documents, theological and ethical tracts, liturgies, and hymns are written in *Ge'ez*, an ancient, unspoken, and largely unknown language. However, a translation of the liturgy and scripture has now been made in *Amharic*, the official language of Ethiopia today.

Typical of Oriental Churches, the Ethiopian Church accepts the authority of the first three ecumenical councils (325 CE, 381 CE, and 431 CE), but explicitly rejects Chalcedon (451 CE).

The Ethiopian Church has *Five Pillars of Mysteries*. These teachings contain the knowledge that each faithful believer should know and understand:

- The Mystery of the Trinity
- The Mystery of the Incarnation
- The Mystery of Baptism
- The Mystery of the Eucharist
- The Mystery of the Resurrection of the Dead

Ethiopia is known as the country of Mary. She is its protector and the nation is her daughter. The Virgin Mary is recognized as the theotokos and is venerated more highly and widely than other saints, called "kedus" or holy. She is honored for her supreme grace and for her response to God's call to bear Jesus. Mary's body does not lie in a grave waiting for a reunion with her soul at the final judgment like the rest of humanity. Instead, at death, she was taken to heaven, body and soul, where she prayers for believers on earth until the Final Judgment. Mary is constantly referred to during the Liturgy. Pictures of Mary are everywhere. Many women and local churches are named for her. The *Nagara Maryam (History of Mary)* is a collection of stories about her life organized and read for the 12 months of the year.

---

[10]See R. W. Cowley, "The Biblical Canon of the Ethiopian Orthodox Church Today," *Ostkirchliche Studien* 23 (1974), pp. 318-323.

## Ways of Living

Because the Ethiopian Church is comprised mostly of Ethiopians, church members follow the social practices common to that culture. Plus, given the strong linkage to Judaism, several practices stemming from that religion may be found in Ethiopia, such as levirate marriage and kosher rules. Women are prohibited from entering a church during menses.

## Ceremonies

Like other Eastern Churches, the Ethiopian community has liturgical worship.

To be a legitimate church, the local congregation must have a *Tabot*, a mini replica of the Ark of the Covenant or at least of one of its stone tablets. Typically, the local bishop gives this fixture. Once a tabot has been removed from the building, it ceases to be seen as a church.

After removing their shoes upon entering a church, men and women sit on separate sides during worship (men on the left and women on the right facing the altar). Women wear white gowns often embroidered with a cross and a large scarf which covers their head (i.e., a shash). These robes cover their street garments. Men wear regular street clothes. During worship, women *Ululate* or warble with a shrill noise.[11] Sometimes, men and women get up from their seats and form a line holding spears that they thrust while they worship. Incense is used, as well as water, which the ornately dressed priest may spray on the congregation. Drums and cymbals (i.e., tseenasele) are employed.

The Ethiopian Church has seven sacraments: Baptism, Penance, Confirmation, Holy Communion, Unction of the Sick, Matrimony, and Holy Orders:

| | |
|---|---|
| • Baptism: | Infants are baptized three times at the church entrance by immersion. Boys are baptized at 40 days after birth, girls at 80 days. |
| • Confirmation: | This ritual takes place immediately after baptism. The priest anoints many locations of the candidate's body with oil (examples include the top of the head, both eyes, and both ears). |

---

[11]To ululate means to make a high-pitched, shrill noise, to hoot, to wail, or to lament loudly. The term itself comes from the Latin word "ululate," meaning to "hoot."

- Confession:

This is strictly a personal ritual. A believer chooses a Confessor-Priest, who knows him intimately. This Confessor is called "Yenafs Abbat" or "Soul-Father." He is the spiritual father to the family, making frequent visits. Yearly, the penitent gives the confessor a gift.

When dying, the penitent calls for the confessor and declares his "nuzazei" or final wishes or will. The Confessor keeps a copy of the will and reads it on the 40th day after death.

- Eucharist:

The bread and wine become the body and blood of Jesus Christ in a mysterious and non-defined way.

- Matrimony:

Marriage of church members by a priest, who anoints the couple with oil several times during the ceremony.

- Unction of the Sick

Prayers for the soul of the sick, which in turn may bring about physical healing.

- Orders

Hands are laid on male candidates for deacon, priest, and bishop. Prayers of consecration and anointing of oil are carried out.

The Ethiopian Orthodox Tewahido Bete Church religious calendar has many movable and immovable holy days and fasts. Some of the major ones include: Christmas, the Baptism of Jesus, Palm Sunday, Holy Week, Ascension Day, and Pentecost. These are all preceded by fasts. For examples, Christmas has Advent (fast for 40 days), and Easter has Lent (fast for 55 days). Other fast days include Nineveh (3 days), Apostles (15 days), and Assumption (15 days).

All baptized members over age seven should fast. During Lent meat and meat products are prohibited.

One of the most important holy days is called *Meskel* (Cross) or "Finding the True Cross" or "Day of the Holy Cross." It is celebrated on September 27th each year. This has taken place for over 1,600 years and it is a major social and religious event in Ethiopian culture. It honors the discovery of the actual cross on which Jesus was crucified by St. Helena, the mother of Constantine the Great, on March 19, 326 CE. The story goes that after the crucifixion, the cross was tossed on a nearby trash heap and that in time it had been covered by more trash, where she found it. St. Helena started a church in Jerusalem on September 27, 326 CE to honor her discovery, hence the day Meskel is actually celebrated. According to Ethiopian tradition, Emperor Zara Yacobe brought the remains of the cross to Ethiopia with great fanfare. This began the annual celebration in Ethiopia.

Typically on the evening of September 26, tall branches are tied together and yellow daisies (meskel flowers) are place on their tops. At night these branches and flowers are gathered in front of crowd of worshippers and ignited, becoming huge bonfires. Crowds dance, chant, and sing around the fires. Joining them are ornately robbed priests carrying silver Coptic crosses. The ignited branches represent the incense that St. Helena used when she asked God to help her find the "true cross." The holiday also remembers the end of the three month rainy season and the return of the sun.[12] The Meskel emphasis on the cross is one of the reasons that Ethiopian Christians have over 1,000 designs for crosses, one of the largest selections in Christendom.

*Lidet* or *Genna* (Christmas) is celebrated on January 6 and 7. This is preceded by an advent fast during which no animal products are consumed. After a long vigil on the evening of Christmas (January 6), a Liturgy is performed at midnight. Christmas Day is traditionally celebrated by visiting friends and relatives. A hockey game (Genna) is often played also.

*Timkat* (Epiphany) celebrates the baptism of Christ in the Jordan River by John the Baptist instead of the visit of the three wise men as celebrated in several other churches. On the day prior to Epiphany, a local church's tabot is removed from its facility and carried to a nearby body of water. Then, it is placed in a tent and the clergy and many lay people perform an all night vigil complete with sung services.

At dawn on Epiphany, the Liturgy of the Holy Mass is sung. After the liturgy, the highest ranking clergy will come out of the tent and bless the waters with a large processional cross, and will float or submerge a lit candle or taper in the water. Lay members present will often jump into the water or

---

[12]Links with nature are part of Meskel celebrations, especially in Southern Ethiopia. There, celebrations last more than one day, perhaps as long as one week. Families come together, buy new clothes, and exchange gifts. Changes in life are recognized (newly wed women march, marriages are arranged). A bull is sacrificed while a man reads prayers and a woman collects the bull's blood, which she dabs on foreheads and places on doorposts, all for blessing and protection.

have the water sprayed on them to obtain a special blessing. Then as priests chant, as bells ring, and drums are beaten, the tabot is taken back to the church buildings in a grand procession of clergy in glittering robes, under embroidered umbrellas, processional crosses, banners, and clouds of incense. The crowd sings, dances, claps, and ululates as it escorts the tabot.

The most significant celebration of Tikat happens at the Axum shrine. A copy of the original tabot, decorated with embroidered green and red velvet cloths, is processed around for about one-half mile. Priests and an honor guard with assault weapons stand in front of the tabot. Women ululate in the rear. Celebrations are normally quite boisterous. The tabot remains inside the tent all night, a symbol of God's presence.

### *Institutions*

Today, the Ethiopian Orthodox Tewahido Church is a non-Chalcedonian community with over 40 to 45 million members (or about one-half of the population of the nation). It is the largest Oriental Orthodox community and is the second largest Eastern Church after the Russian Orthodox. *Tewahido* means "made one." This emphasizes the non-Chalcedonian teaching that the divinity and the humanity of Christ are forever united. In many ways, the Ethiopian Church has been merely a protégée of the Coptic Church for centuries. However, it became independent (i.e., an autocephalous Patriarchate) in a 1948 CE agreement with the Coptic church.

The church is divided by dioceses, each with a bishop. The patriarch of the Ethiopian Orthodox Tewahido Church is called an *Abuna* (Our Father). Prior to 1951 CE, abunas came from the Coptic Church. Since that time, the church has ordained Ethiopian abunas. This leader is the spiritual and temporal head of the church after the fall of the monarchy in 1974 CE.

There are several categories of clergy, collectively labeled the *Kahinat*. Included in the kahinat are priests, deacons, monks, and the debteras.

A male between the ages of seven and ten who desires to become a deacon begins to attend a church school and lives with a teacher—a priest or debtera who is especially learned. Yet, most priests come from peasant lineage and their education is limited.

After four years of study, the local bishop ordains the man a deacon. After three or four years of study and service, the deacon can be ordained a priest. If this is allowed, he must get married prior to ordination or remain celibate to remain ritually pure. Marriage after priesting, divorce, or adultery makes a man impure and thus unsuitable for ordination.

Though not ordained, debteras assist by chanting the church services in Ge'ez. These individuals may have chosen not to pursue ordination or they may no longer be considered ritually pure enough to be deacons or priests. They often have a wider range of learning and skills than what is necessary for priests. Debteras can be choristers, poets, herbalists, astrologers, fortune-tellers, and scribes.

Monks are either ordained priests or laymen. They are typically widowers with the time to commit themselves to a pious life. Some monks are celibate, having chosen that when young. They often commit themselves to gaining advanced religious education. Monks may live a hermit's life or may live in the church's monastic communities.

The church has a small number of nuns. They most likely live in community and have to have priests to carry out the Eucharist. Daily living for nuns may include prayer and devotions, study, and social service (to a limited degree).[13]

All clergy are ordained in apostolic succession through a line of bishops traced back to the original apostles.

## SEE WHAT YOU KNOW ABOUT EASTERN ORIENTAL CHRISTIANITY

1. Identify and describe four beliefs.

2. Identify and describe three characteristics of lifestyle.

---

[13] For an unusual life story and contemporary music ministry of one Ethiopian nun, see "Historic Concert by Ethiopian Nun and Composer in D.C.," *Tadis* (July 8, 2008), http://www.tadias.com/2008/07/08/historic-concert-by-ethiopian-nun-pianist-composer-in-dc/

For more information on Ethiopian Orthodox nuns, see Marta C. Wright, "At the Limits of Sexuality: The Femininity of Ethiopian Orthodox Nuns." *Journal of Ethiopian Studies* 35:1 (2002), pp. 27-42.

3. Identify and describe four characteristics of ceremonies.

4. Identify and describe three characteristics of institutions.

# CHAPTER IV

## ✠

# EASTERN ORTHODOX CHRISTIANITY

Eastern Orthodox Churches are those communities of faith that are in communion with the Patriarch of Constantinople. The dizzying array of names for these churches and for their leaders can be baffling to outsiders. The following are considered Eastern Orthodox Churches:

- The Great Church:
  This community is headed by the Patriarch of Constantinople himself and takes precedence over all others. It covers Turkey and Asia Minor. Under the Patriarch of Constantinople are 74 *Metropolitans* and 20 other bishops.

- Alexandria:
  With 4 metropolitans, this church includes all Orthodox communities in Egypt.

- Antioch:
  With 12 metropolitans and 2 or 3 bishops, this community takes in churches from an area bordered by Syria, Palestine, Constantinople, and the Euphrates River.

- Jerusalem:
  This church includes all Orthodox communities in Palestine with 13 metropolitans.

- Cyprus:  A small church, merely the island.

- Russia:  The largest group with a *Holy Synod* of 3 metropolitans, the *Exarch* of Georgia, and 5 to 6 other bishops or *Archimandrites*. There are 86 dioceses and missionary bishops in Siberia, Japan, and North America.

- Carlovitz:  Orthodox Serbs in Hungary with 6 *Sees*.

- Czernagora:  One independent diocese in the Black Mountain.

- The Church of Sinai:  One monastery with a *Hegumenos* as archbishop.

- The Greek Church:  Thirty-two sees with a Holy Synod.

- Hermannstadt:  The Church of the Vlachs in Hungary with 3 sees.

- The Bulgarian Church:  Under the exarch who lives in Constantinople. In Bulgaria there are 11 sees with a Holy Synod.

- Czernovitz:  Four sees over the Orthodox in Austria.

- Serbia:  The Serbian National Church with four sees.

- Rumania:  A national church with a Holy Synod and eight sees.

- Herzegovina and Bosnia:  Four sees that are very independent with a vague recognition of Constantinople.[1]

---

[1] A see is the headquarters or "seat" of a bishop (i.e., or whatever title used for this role). A synod is a church meeting, composed of some combination of bishops, clergy, and/or lay people.

## The Russian Orthodox Church

The Russian Orthodox Church of the Moscow Patriarchate or the Orthodox Christian Church of Russia is a group of Christians under the authority of the Patriarch of Moscow.[2] This patriarch is in communion with the Patriarch of Constantinople and all churches linked with him. The Russian Church has 135 million people worldwide and about 29,000 churches. It is the second largest church in the world after the Roman Catholic community.

Beginning with the fall of Tsarism in 1917 CE, the church endured harsh persecution that resulted not only in the loss of political power, but even more important, the loss of human beings and facilities. It has only recently begun to recover.[3]

---

The following definitions will hopefully shed some light on name for leaders in Eastern Orthodoxy:

Patriarch: Derived from the Latin word "pater" or father. In the Eastern faith, the title is given to the head bishops of Constantinople, Alexandria, Antioch, Jerusalem, Moscow, Serbia, and Romania.

Ecumenical Patriarch: Reserved for the Patriarch of Constantinople, who is the chief authority in the Eastern Orthodox faith.

Exarch: Ranking second in authority, derived from the Latin word "exarchus" and Greek "exarkhos" or leader, a bishop ranking immediately beneath a patriarch.

Metropolitan: Derived from the Latin word "metropolitanus" or resident of a metropolis, a bishop who ranks beneath the patriarch who has authority over an ecclesiastical province and other bishops.

Hegumenos: Derived from the Latin word "hegumenus" or leader, the head of a religious community or monastery.

Archimandrites: Derived from the Latin word "archimandrites" or monastery or cattle pen, the head of a monastery or group of monasteries, equivalent to an abbot.

Bishop: Derived from the Latin word "episcopus," meaning guardian or overseer, a clergyperson normally in charge of a diocese and its churches and priests.

[2] For more information on the Russian Orthodox Church, see its official website http://www.mospat.ru

[3] For more information on this human tragedy, see Roslof, Edward, *Red Priests: Renovationism, Russian Orthodoxy, and Revolution, 1905-1946* (Bloomington, Indiana, 2002); Husband, William B, *"Godless Communists": Atheism and Society in Soviet Russia* (DeKalb: Northern Illinois University Press, 2000); Peris, Daniel, *Storming the Heavens: The Soviet League of the Militant Godless* (Ithaca: Cornell University Press, 1998); Young, Glennys, *Power and the Sacred in Revolutionary Russia: Religious Activists in the Village* (University Park: Pennsylvania State University Press, 1997); Pospielovsky, Dimitry V., *A History of Marxist-Leninist Atheism and Soviet Anti-Religious Policies* (New York; St. Martin's Press, 1987); idem, *The Russian Church Under the Soviet Regime 1917-1982* (St. Vladimir's Seminary Press, 1984); Ellis, Jane, *The Russian Orthodox Church: A Contemporary History* (Bloomington: Indiana University Press, 1986); and, Curtis, John Shelton, *The Russian Church and the Soviet State* (Boston: Little Brown, 1953).

This church should not be mistaken with the *Russian Orthodox Church Outside Russia* (also known as ROCOR or the Russian Orthodox Church Abroad).[4] After years of separation, the two churches reconciled through the Act of Canonical Communion, signed on May 17, 2007 CE. Immediately following, the Divine Liturgy was celebrated in Moscow. The Patriarch of Moscow and All Russia Alexius II and the First Hierarch of ROCOR concelebrated for the first time in history.[5]

### Beliefs

Similar to other Orthodox Churches, the Russian Orthodox Church stresses maintaining ancient doctrines and practices as opposed to adapting these to modern times. The faithful take pride in the fact that what they believe and practice are similar to what existed 1,000 years ago.

### Ceremonies

*Church Slavonic* is used in a majority of religious ceremonies, although modern Russian may be used in sermons.

Russian Orthodox Church buildings differ in design from many western type churches. First, Russian Orthodox churches are built in a *Cruciform* with the altar facing east. Also, they have a three-fold division of narthex, nave, and altar. Third, their interiors are enhanced with many sacramental objects, including holy icons, which are hung on the walls or may be free-standing.

Found in the sanctuary, the altar is separated from the nave by a stone, wood, or metal screen called an *Iconostasis*. The iconostasis has three doors often called Royal Gates and two Deacon's Doors. It is usually two or three steps higher than the floor of the nave and set back a few steps. The iconostasis does not normally go to the top of the church. This allows the congregation to hear the chanting of priests when they stand behind the iconostasis.

The central or Royal Gates (or Holy Doors or Beautiful Gates) are usually closed when services are not being held. If and when they are open or shut during services varies by local custom.

Side doors are normally called Deacon's Doors or Angel's Doors. They may be called the former due to the fact that deacons use these and often icons of sainted deacons cover them (most noticeably, St. Stephen the Pro-

---

[4] The Russian Orthodox Church Abroad was formed by Russian communities outside Communist Russia. Members refused to recognize the authority of the Russian Orthodox Church because they believed that the Bolshevik government controlled the church. The Church has over 400 parishes worldwide, and an estimated membership of over 400,000 people. Within the ROCOR there are 13 hierarchs, and also 20 monasteries and nunneries in the United States, Canada, Australia, New Zealand, Germany, the United Kingdom, and South America.

[5] However, this reconciliation has been controversial. Many ROCOR parishes have refused to recognize the reunion with the Moscow Patriarchate, and others have taken steps to shield their property from the Patriarchate.

tomarytr and St. Ephrem the Syrian). They may be labeled Angel's Doors when they are covered with depictions of Michael and Gabriel, two biblical archangels.

Special icons are located in accordance with tradition going upward and standing facing toward the front:

| | |
|---|---|
| • The Bottom Tier or Sovereign: | On either side of the Beautiful Gates are icons of Jesus Christ (right side) and the Virgin Mary (left side). Other icons on each side might be the patron saint or feast day of the local church and/or one or more of the 12 Apostles. Above this are two transposable levels: the Deisis or the Twelve Great Feasts. |
| • The Deisis: | In the center of this, is an icon of Christ on a throne. On either side is an icon of John the Baptist and the Virgin Mary. Beyond these are icons of Michael and/or Gabriel, Peter, Paul or or any Church Father(s) chosen. |
| • The Feasts: | This level contains icons of the 12 feasts of the church yearly calendar. |
| • Two Other Tiers: | These are interchangeable. One tier includes Old Testament prophets and patriarchs, including the sons of Jacob. These are found on either side of the "Our Lady of the Sign" (a Virgin Mary icon that depicts the Annunciation or the time when Mary was told she would bear Jesus). The other tier includes the 12 Apostles, and/or the Trinity. |

It is not unusual to find an icon of the *Mystical Supper*, a depiction the Last Supper and the Communion of Saints in the Kingdom of God above the Beautiful Gates.

The Sovereign level is always present. Other tiers may or may not be found depending on the size and elaborateness of the local church.

The icon screen normally reaches to the inside top of the dome (or domes). On the ceiling of many churches (inside the main dome) is an icon of *Christ as Pantokrator* (Ruler of All). These icons stress Christ's humanity and divinity, pointing out that Christ is a man and yet also God.

In Russia, most churches are lit with candles rather than electric light. Virtually all churches have votive candle stands in front of the icons. Beeswax candles are used. The wax and oil are symbolic of the purity and sincerity of the gifts that provide them.

Typically, worshippers purchase candles in church stores, light them up, and place them on the stands. This ceremony demonstrates a person's prayer to God, the Holy Mother, or to the saints or angels.

A large crucifix with a painted image of Christ is placed to the left of the church. This image has candles placed before it in memory of those who have died.

There are very clear rules about who and when a person may enter or leave the sanctuary and by which doors. Bishops are permitted to enter the Beautiful Gates at any time. Priests and deacons can enter these doors when they are open during services. Lay people cannot go through the doors or be in the altar/sanctuary area unless they are assisting in services. The altar/sanctuary area is closed to anyone outside of services unless there is a reason. To go into this area, a lay person has a blessing. Women are not allowed to enter the altar/sanctuary area.[6]

Generally, there are no pews, although some American churches have added them. Normally, people stand or kneel during the liturgy, out of respect for the presence of God. Some folding chairs for the elderly and ill are located along the walls, but people stand if they can when the Royal Gates are open. Women only wear dresses or skirts and many often cover their heads. Men remove their hats.

Icons and people are covered with incense. This symbolizes the grace of the Holy Spirit, which is given to all people. The censer, or "kadilo," stands for Christ, the Divine Ember.

Instead of using musical instruments, the faithful sing hymns and responses to the chanting of a priest in an a cappella fashion.

People make the sign of the cross with the thumb and first two fingers of the right hand joined at the tips with the third and fourth fingers closed at the palm. They touch the brow, the breast, the right shoulder, and the left shoulder, signifying that a person's mind, heart, soul, and strength are dedicated to God. When the priest or bishop blesses the people, his fingers are held to form the Greek letters "IC XC," the first and last letters of Jesus Christ.

In communion, the priest places a small piece of prosfir, or blessed bread, in a single chalice filled with wine. Believers then receive this wine-

---

[6] There are some exceptions to these rules. For example, when a male child is "churched," he is brought by the priest into the altar/sanctuary area to be dedicated.

soaked bread by means of a common spoon. Prior to communion, an individual must go to confession. This is done either before the liturgy or the night before, and the communicant must have fasted since midnight.

Children receive chrismation at baptism and may receive communion without confession or fasting until the *Age of Reason.*

### Institutions

The Russian Orthodox Church is organized into geographic areas called eparchies or dioceses. Each diocese contains parishes. Every local building and membership is called a prikhod. Besides local parishes and dioceses, the church has a number of monasteries, which have played a significant role in the life of the church since its founding.[7]

Hierarchical in structure, the Russian Orthodox Church is headed by the *Patriarch of Moscow and All Russia,* head of the Moscow Patriarchate. He is considered the "first among equals" (i.e., with other bishops of the Russian Church). On February 1, 2009 CE, the church "enthroned" its first patriarch since the fall of Communism and restoration of religious freedoms in the former Soviet Union. The new patriarch's name is *Kirill I* or *Cyril I* (his secular name is Vladimir Mikhailovich Gundyayev).

Along with the Patriarch of Moscow and All Russia, other bishops form the highest rank in the church and are leaders of priests.

A few eparchies constitute exarchates or autonomous churches. Currently these include the Orthodox Churches of Belarusia, the Latvian, the Moldavian, and the Estonian Orthodox Church. Although autonomous, these churches are in communion with the Patriarch of Moscow and All Russia and in that with the Patriarch of Constantinople.[8]

Each local church has a priest. Prior to ordination, priests may marry. If widowed, a priest may not remarry (a bishop is either a widower or has never married).

Even though the Patriarch of Moscow and All Russia has wide-ranging powers, he has limitations. Unlike the Roman Pope, he is not considered infallible.[9] A council of bishops, for example, handles matters of faith and practice (i.e., *Pomestny Sobor*).[10]

---

[7] For an example of this significant role, see Jennifer Jean Wynot, *Keeping the Faith: Russian Orthodox Monasticism in the Soviet Union, 1917-1939,* Eastern European Studies 27 (College Station: Texas A & M University Press, 2004).

[8] Chinese and Japanese Orthodox churches have been given full autonomy by the Russian Orthodox Church, although that independence is not always recognized.

[9] See Chapter Five for more details on this subject.

[10] However, there are some issues that cannot be decided inside the Russian Church itself, they must be settled by a general council of all Orthodox churches. For example, a 787 CE Council settled the issue of icons. For more information, see "Iconoclastic Controversy," http://atheism.about.com/library/glossary/western/bldef_iconoclastic.htm

### SEE WHAT YOU KNOW ABOUT EASTERN ORTHODOX CHRISTIANITY

1. Identify and describe four beliefs.

2. Identify and describe three characteristics of lifestyle.

3. Identify and describe four characteristics of ceremonies.

4. Identify and describe three characteristics of institutions.

# CHAPTER V
✠
# ROMAN CATHOLIC CHRISTIANITY

*Introduction*

The Roman Catholic branch of Christendom can best be defined *Organizationally*: all the churches and individuals in the world that are under the spiritual authority of the Bishop of Rome, also called the Pope, the Pontiff, or Holy Father. Using an organizational definition is important for Roman Catholics. This is because they stress the central role that the *Institution* has in the life of the devout Roman Catholic believer. The central role of the institution can be found in everything Roman Catholics believe and practice.

*Roman* refers to the city of Rome and its bishop, and *Catholic* can be defined as "universal." The Roman Catholic Community is comparable to a large wheel with spokes all surrounding the hub. The hub is the Bishop of Rome, the spokes are the various communities that feed into it (communities like the Roman Catholic Churches of the United States or the Philippines, for example). These all form one whole piece. Merely calling this branch of Christendom catholic is insufficient. There are several universal churches, but only one has a headquarters in Rome, Italy.

There are approximately 1.141 billion Roman Catholics in the world with 408,000 priests and almost 3,000 dioceses. Roman Catholics make up about ¼ of the population of the United States and are the largest religious community found here (65-70 million members).

Quickly rising numbers of Spanish speaking followers are changing the ethnic make-up of the American Roman Catholic church and are impacting practice. Hispanic Roman Catholics are bringing a more emotional and traditional, almost pre-Vatican II style to the church.[1]

---

[1] See Thomas Russell, "Latino Roman Catholicism Music City Style!, Presentation for the Latina/o Religion, Culture and Society Group, American Academy of Religion Annual Meeting, November 24, 2003; and "Factbox: America's Roman Catholic

The current Roman Catholic Church has been influenced by *Vatican* ii to a great extent. Held between 1962-65 CE, this international meeting's purpose was to update the church. Vatican ii transformed the church in too many ways to count. It permitted churches to use the vernacular language of the people instead of the universal use of Church Latin. In the United States, English began to be used, in Spain, Spanish, and so on. Because of Vatican ii, the Roman Catholic Church began to view other religions in a new light. Previously, the church had taught that no religious truth could be found outside the Roman Catholic Church. This meant that Eastern and Protestant Christians as well as non-Christian religious practitioners had nothing of truth in their religions. Since Vatican ii, the church has taught that it has the fullness of religious truth. This left a small door open for finding some religious truth in other traditions.

As a result, the Roman Catholic Church has involved itself in ecumenical discussions with other Christians and with non-Christians often way ahead of many other Christian bodies. Also, Vatican ii gave lay people more responsibility for parish life and encouraged Bible study.

However, Vatican ii fostered a number of reactions among Roman Catholics themselves. Many regret that Vatican ii and its reforms ever occurred. These *Pre-Vatican* ii or Traditionalist Roman Catholics hope for a restoration of the liturgical forms, public and private devotions, and presentation of Roman Catholic teachings that prevailed in the Church before the Second Vatican Council. They want the Mass to be said in Latin and believe that priests have lost some of their authority. In recent years, the traditionalist position has "gone public" because of the popularity of the film, *The Passion of the Christ*, and its creator, actor Mel Gibson, a traditionalist Roman Catholic.[2]

Traditionalist ideas are also depicted in the recent movie, *While You Were Sleeping*, when Gladys Johns, playing a grandmother at Mass, says, "When did they change the Mass from Latin? I liked it so much better when you didn't understand what the priest was saying."[3]

On the other hand, many *Post-Vatican* ii church members long for more reforms along Vatican ii lines and struggle against members from the other group. They prefer the Mass said in the vernacular and they welcome the new roles for lay people. Some Post-Vatican ii Roman Catholics want to see a liberalization of church social policies, in particular the roles for women as ordained clergy.

---

Population" (April 10, 2008), http://www.reuters.com/article/newsOne/idUSN 0945928720080410

[2] *The Passion of the Christ* (2004 CE). For more information on Mel Gibson and his traditional Roman Catholicism, see Michael G. Lawler, "Sectarian Catholicism and Mel Gibson," *Journal of Religion and Film* 8:1 Special Issue (February 2004).

[3] Sandra Bullock and Bill Pullman co-starred in this 1995 romantic comedy produced by Caravan Pictures.

A story best explains the Pre- and Post-Vatican II conflict. In the late 1980s CE, a Roman Catholic woman in Nashville, Tennessee joined a Bible study of Roman Catholic women led by a Protestant woman. She loved the Bible study and was encouraged by her local priest to dig into the Bible more for herself. A few months later, this woman moved to a new city and joined a new parish. She went to her new priest and told him how excited she was studying the Bible in the group and on her own. In no uncertain words, the priest told her that she should not attend Bible studies or study the Bible on her own unless directed by a priest. It was the church and priest's role to explain the Bible. After this conversation, she went down the street and joined another Roman Catholic parish with a priest like the one she had had in Nashville.

### Beliefs

One feature of the Roman Catholic faith is its belief about final authority. In simple terms, what or who are the final authorities that determine what is correct belief and practice?

This branch of Christendom teaches that the *Bible and the Church and its Tradition up to this Moment* should be the authorities for belief and practice. The Roman Catholic Bible includes all books common to all three branches of Christendom plus the Apocrypha. The notion of "the church and its tradition up to this moment" refers to anything that the church writes or pronounces. This includes hymns, theological writings (such as Thomas Aquinas), and canon or church law.

The further aspect of final authority flows directly from the previous beliefs. According to Roman Catholic teaching, the church acts as an official interpreter of the Bible and tradition. The church has the *Magisterium* or "teaching authority," which carries out this function. The Roman Catholic argument is that without the guiding role of the Church in biblical interpretation, all sorts of problems can emerge. The Church says, "Look at the tragedies of Waco and Jonestown, both Protestant groups. We don't have those kinds of problems because the Church is the guardian of truth and protector of the faithful."

The crucial role that saints like Mary, the Mother of Jesus, play in the life of the faithful is stressed by Roman Catholics. They believe that saints, like the Mother Theresas of history, do not cease to be influential just because they are dead. A Roman Catholic will say, "Why waste a bunch of good dead people?"[4]

---

[4] Deceased Christians that deserve special honor are remembered by the three Christian traditions in different ways. The Roman Catholic view is noted above. In the Eastern tradition, saints are identified, honored, and venerated. Churches and individuals are named after them. They have special holy days. Given the diverse nature of Protestantism, there is great variety in how these special people are handled. Some Protestants think like Roman Catholics, some like Eastern Christians, and some ignore them altogether. However, even those in the last category remember special

Individuals are officially recognized as saints by means of a three-stage process. First, at the local level, Christians come to believe that a person of special holiness has lived in their community (i.e., the person has died). The story of this individual's life is told over and over again and may even be printed in a book. A small group is established to spread the news about this would-be saint. Christians begin to pray to the person and their prayers may be answered. Miraculous signs may also occur.

Eventually, the local bishop may be asked to launch the official process toward sainthood. If the bishop sees merit in the request, he organizes a committee of experts to investigate the person's life, faith, and holiness. Individuals who knew the individual are interviewed. Potential miracles are verified. Finally, the bishop asks other bishops about the candidate's viability.

The second stage, beatification, begins when the local bishop gives the materials collected about the person to the Vatican's Congregation for the Causes of Saints. Using these, officials create a historical-critical biography of the potential saint's life and piety. Of particular significance is the historical context of the individual. Did he or she meet a challenge that they overcame by faith in their time and place? Did they live a life of noticeable holiness and piety? Did they die a martyr? If the potential saint was martyred, a miracle attributed to them after their death is unnecessary. If they person did not die as a martyr, a miracle attributed to them after their death must be established by officials.

In either case, the Pope can declare that beatification can proceed after a panel of theological experts judges the candidate worthy. The actual declaration proclaims that the person is one of the blessed and worthy of public honor. After beatification, the individual can be called blessed.

*Canonization* is the third and final stage in the process toward sainthood. In this stage, the church adds the individual's name to the list or canon of officially recognized Roman Catholic saints.

To achieve canonization, a person must have another authentic miracle attributed to them after death. Then if the candidate's reputation for holiness continues to spread throughout the world, the Pope may choose to canonize.

The Roman Catholic Church does not claim that its list of saints is exhaustive. The church teaches that those designated as saints are witnesses to God's grace at work throughout all time and in all places. Saints serve as examples of how to follow Jesus Christ. Citing Hebrews 12:1, the Roman Catholic faith feels that there are too many unrecognized saints to count. ("Since we are surrounded by so great a cloud of witnesses. . ."). Saints have been "de-sainted" when new information arises that disproves their holiness.

A simple line sums up the Roman Catholic view of saints, "Jesus saves you and saints aid you." In other words, a person's sins are forgiven only

---

heroes of the faith. Biographies of these individuals, especially missionaries, line church library walls and can be found in Protestant Christian bookstores.

through the atoning death of Jesus, but saints can assist the faithful in daily living by dispensing non-saving grace and by answering prayer. A great deal of devotional life surrounds the saints, but they are not worshipped. Saints are venerated instead. This means that the faithful Roman Catholic shows respect for the saint.[5]

The most important saint is Mary, the mother of Jesus. Mary is given days for remembering her piety and Roman Catholics name their children after her.

The Roman Catholic tradition has some special doctrines for Mary to preserve her special role as the mother of Jesus. These teachings are a way of answering the question: "How could an imperfect human being (i.e., Mary) give birth and mother a perfect son (i.e., Jesus)?

In 1854 CE, the Church gave its answer by declaring that she was born without any "stain" of original sin (i.e., the *Immaculate Conception*) and in 1950 CE, by asserting that at death, Mary's body and soul immediately went to heaven (i.e., *Bodily Assumption of Mary*).[6]

Almost all traditional branches of Christianity teach that after death, the forgiven soul goes to be with God in heaven. The un-forgiven soul is eternally separated from God and goes to hell.

Different than other branches, the Roman Church adds a third destination, *Purgatory*.[7] Purgatory is not a place where the deceased have a second chance to accept God's grace in Christ and then go to be with God instead of hell. This third location is not a permanent abode. The Church teaches that the soul bound for hell goes directly to hell. On the other hand, souls bound for heaven will end up there. Some go directly, while others go to purgatory to purge remaining sins from their lives.

Two illustrations help to explain this concept to non-Roman Catholics. First, purgatory is somewhat like the experience of Dorothy, Toto, the Scare-

---

[5] For more information on Roman Catholic saints, see Kenneth Woodward, *Making Saints* (New York: Simon and Schuster, 1997).

[6] For the dogma of the Immaculate Conception, Roman Catholics cite Genesis 3:15, Song of Solomon 4:7, Luke 1:28, and several early church theologians as support for this doctrine.

For the dogma of the Bodily Assumption of Mary, Roman Catholics cite Psalm 45:9-17, Psalm 132:8, Song of Songs 3:6, 4:8, 6:9 and 8:5, Isaiah 60:13, Luke 1:28, John 14:3, I Corinthians 15:21-26, and Revelation 12:1-2.

Generally speaking at death, Christians believe that the body and soul separate. The body lies in the grave and the soul goes to be with God. At the final judgment, the body and soul are reunited for eternity and are with God. For more information, see http://www.desiringgod.org/ResourceLibrary/Articles/ByDate/2006/1431_What _happens_at_death/

[7] Roman Catholic justification for purgatory comes from the following Bible passages: Matthew 12:32; I Corinthians 3:10-15; Hebrews 12:29; Revelation 21:27; 1 Peter 3:19, and 2 Maccabees 12:44-46.

crow, the Lion, and the Tin Woodsman of the *Wizard of Oz*. The intrepid four, plus the dog could not meet with the wizard when they first arrived in the Emerald City because they were not prepared to do so. Each had to be "gussied up." Dorothy, Toto, and the Lion had their hair done. The Scarecrow was given more straw and the Tin Woodsman had his dented tin pounded out and he was freshly oiled. All were cleaned up and prepared to meet the wizard.

A second illustration goes as follows: Pretend that Mother Theresa and Adolph Hitler died at the same time and also pretend that both were devout Roman Catholics at the moment of death (easy to say for the former, but a deathbed confession for the latter is a stretch). If no purgatory exists, the two would walk hand-in-hand into God's presence immediately. Instead, purgatory would be a necessary stop for Hitler.[8]

These examples demonstrate that a saved soul needs further cleansing before facing God (or the wizard). This is the reason for Purgatory.

### Roman Catholic Ways of Life

Roman Catholic ways of living or *Moral Theology* is concerned with the moral judgments of human beings, how people ought to behave, and the minimum standards individuals must try to obtain.

There are several concepts that are crucial to understanding Roman Catholicism's approach to living. First and foremost is the community's understanding of the concept of the church. That is, the church is the final authority in matters of what to believe and practice. Another way of saying this is that the Roman Catholic communion believes that the Bible and tradition until right now are equal in authority over the lives of its members.

But, why is the church the final authority? Roman Catholics believe that God established this institution to dispense zaps of grace and to guide, teach, and protect the faithful. To the devout, the presence of the church is significant because without this institution there would be chaos. Roman Catholics point to all the cults that have emerged from Protestantism to demonstrate that a movement without a single, final human authority creates theological disarray.

How does the Roman Catholic Church contribute to ethical living? It gives the sacraments that provide zaps of grace for the faithful so that they can live right. In baptism, an infusion of grace sets them on the path to live morally, in the Eucharist, regular zaps of grace sustains the faithful, and in penance, grace cleanses the soul after confession so that the devout can live a holier life. The church also has the Magisterium, whose function it is to evaluate new doctrines and practices and guide and/or protect the faithful.

---

[8] For more details on Mother Theresa, see Mother Theresa and Brian Kolodiejchuk, ed., *Mother Theresa: Come Be My Light: The Private Writings of the Saint of Calcutta* (New York: Doubleday, 2007).

One leader is the head of the church and although he is fallible, human, and a titular head, not a dictator, he is the head pastor or shepherd of the communion. There are times that he might speak infallibly, but only after the church has worked through an issue. The church has *Canon Law* and its own court system. The former is a body of legal codes that help direct the faithful.

The church has communities of *Monks* and *Nuns* that help individuals live holy lives and serve as examples to the rest of the faithful how to live righteously. Monks and nuns also help the community around them become more ethical through their teaching and social service.

Finally, the church releases *Encyclicals*, which are statements about moral issues, such as worker's rights, abortion, relating to non-Christians, and the use of artificial means of birth control. The Roman Catholic Communion has had a lengthy history of making statements about social justice, especially in the past 100 years. The following seven principles highlight some of the major themes from Catholic social-teaching documents of the last century:

- Dignity of the Human Person:

  All people are sacred, made in the image and likeness of God. People do not lose dignity due to disability, poverty, age, or race. This emphasizes people over things, being over having.

- Community and the Common Good:

  The human person is both sacred and social. We realize our dignity and rights in relationship with others, in community.

- Rights and Responsibility:

  People have fundamental rights to life, food, shelter, health care, education, and employment. Corresponding with these rights are duties to respect the rights of others in the wider society and to work for the common good.

- Option for the Poor:

  The moral test of a society is how it treats its most vulnerable members. We are called to look at public policy decisions in terms of how they affect the poor.

- Dignity of Work: People have the right to decent and productive work, fair wages, private property, and economic initiative. The economy exists to serve people, not the other way around.

- Solidarity: We are a human family. Our responsibilities to each other cross national, racial, economic, and ideological differences. We are called to work globally for peace.

- Care for God's Creation: The goods of the earth are gifts from God. We have a responsibility to care for these goods as stewards and trustees, not as mere consumers and users.[9]

Another trait that marks Roman Catholic Moral Theology is its *Internationalism.* While the church makes general pronouncements supposedly for the global community, exactly how these pronouncements are handled differ by geographically.

This is exemplified by a large, looming issue throughout the Roman Catholic world concerning the final authority of the church versus local autonomy. In certain countries, the devout feel that they can disagree with the church and still be a faithful member. In North America, the faithful feel that a true believer can use artificial means of birth control and still be true to faith, whereas in other sections of the Roman Catholic world, this would be sacrilegious. However, even in those nations, which are more conservative or more liberal, there are strong opposing factions.

*Natural Law* is an important concept in Roman Catholic ethics. It is the God-established "normal" way of doing things that everyone, Christian or not, recognizes. Christians should discover this law in operation and "go with the flow." The church often uses natural law arguments for ethical teachings. For example, abortion is wrong because it interrupts the natural flow of prenatal human development. The same is true for artificial means of birth control, which artificially stops the natural creation of a human being. Part of this aspect of Roman Catholic ethical teaching involves a *Consistent Life Ethic.* The church has been opposed to anything that takes life unnaturally, ranging from abortion and infanticide to the development and use of nuclear weapons.

---

[9] For more information, see http://www.usccb.org/sdwp/projects/socialteaching/excerpt.shtml

Roman Catholics are divided about what role women should play in their church. As a whole, the faithful admire the significant role women have played in the history of their church. Many have become nuns and been involved in education, social service, and pastoral care. Mother Theresa of Calcutta, Mother Elizabeth Bayley Seton, and Dorothy Day immediately come to mind. Current debate surrounds abortion rights, the use of artificial means of birth control, the ordination of women as priests, and marriage/divorce concerns. Although the church has official teachings on all these matters, there are considerable debates about them and disagreement with the church, especially in the United States.[10]

Large numbers of Roman Catholic children attend church-related educational institutions or *Parochial Schools*. The term parochial in a general sense refers to those schools that include religious education as part of standard curriculums. Or, the term is used for schools run by local dioceses or parishes. In the United States, in particular, the term refers to Roman Catholic institutions as opposed to secular ones.

According to the National Catholic Education Association, in the United States there are:

- 7.6 million students in Roman Catholic schools on all levels, including
- higher education
- 2,320,651 students in elementary, middle, and high schools
- 7,498 schools (6,288 elementary schools, 1,210 high schools)[11]

In surveys, Roman Catholics choose parochial schools for four reasons:

- To provide for faith formation
- To have high academic standards
- To have values-added education
- To provide for a safe school environment[12]

While these numbers are down from previous years, they do still suggest that parochial education is important to many Roman Catholics. Their numbers

---

[10] For good resources on the issue of women's ordination, see:

Anti-women's ordination, Michael Tortolani, "Why No Women's Ordination" at http://www.catholic.com/thisrock/1996/9601fea3.asp

Pro-women's ordination (and some anti-women's ordination), "The Roman Catholic Church and Female Ordination" at http://www.religioustolerance.org/femclrg1.htm

[11] http://www.ncea.org/FAQ/CatholicEducationFAQ.asp

[12] http://www.ncea.org/FAQ/CatholicEducationFAQ.asp

are much higher than any other religiously affiliated educational system in the world.

## *Ceremonies*

Local churches in the Roman tradition have certain common features. Roman Catholicism is a visual faith. Members employ a variety of physical objects as part of their worship. They pray using rosary beads and pray with *relics*, objects or body parts of saints.[13] Clergy wear robes that mimic clothes worn by men and women in the ancient Greco-Roman world. The priest wears a long white garment or alb, a chasuble (over the alb), and a stole (a long piece of cloth about four inches wide draped around the neck).

Church buildings generally have the following characteristics:

- Entering the church (the narthex):

A baptismal font and/or pool and a bowl of holy water is positioned near the entrance. Standing by the pool is a paschal candle, a large candle representing the sacrifice of Christ. Also present is a small niche in the wall, an ambry, which contains three vessels of oil (oil of catechumens to bless those preparing for baptism; oil of the sick; and the sacred chrism, which is used in baptism, confirmation and holy orders). In newer churches, there is a reconciliation chapel for the celebration of the sacrament of reconciliation (Confession). Confessional booths are sometimes present. These small cubicles contain a place for a priest to sit, separated by a screen or grill where the penitent kneels or sits to confess sins.

- The assembly area (the nave)

The nave is normally filled with pews or chairs (older churches in Europe may have neither). Kneelers may also be present. Around the walls of the church normally are the Stations of the Cross. These are depictions of

---

[13] The Roman Catholic Church cites Acts 5:15 and 19:11-12 to support the use of relics.

last events of Jesus' life. The faithful go from station to station (1-14) and reflect on these events as a devotional act.

• The sanctuary:

The focal point for sacred action is the sanctuary and it contains the presider's chair, the lectern, and the altar. In the chief church of the diocese this chair is called the cathedra or bishop's chair, hence the term cathedral. There is also a lectern (which is sometimes called the ambo or pulpit). The word lectern is more commonly used because it is the place where the lectionary is placed and read. The lectionary is the book of readings from the Bible that are prescribed for each service. Preaching can be done from any position. The altar is where the Lord's Supper is celebrated. It is an altar of sacrifice and a banquet table for the Eucharist. When the Eucharist is celebrated the table is covered by an altar cloth. Bread on a bread plate or paten and wine in a chalice are placed on the table also. There is always a cross or crucifix in the area.

• The tabernacle:

Tabernacles or "little houses" are used to hold the left-over sacrament. They have small golden doors and are placed on the altar with a red lamp burning before it. In recent years, the tabernacle has been moved to a Eucharistic chapel.

• Candles, statues:

Reredos (statues, paintings, and carved shrines) can be found along the walls behind altars or the side walls in older parishes. These serve as worship aids. Stained glass windows, which depict Jesus and other biblical characters, may also be present. Candles are important. There is a sanctuary lamp before the tabernacle, votive candles in front of a statue or shrine lit in prayer, and a variety of other candles in many places. These may have no religious significance at all, but merely have been retained from the time when they provided light.

Roman Catholicism is a liturgical community of faith with seven sacraments. Even though there are minor cultural differences that impact practice, the community's core rituals remain the same throughout the world.[14]

The term sacrament is employed because Roman Catholics believe the participant receives a zap of grace in the ritual itself and people are changed inwardly and spiritually. Sacraments are considered efficacious or effective in themselves because grace comes through the act, regardless of the person officiating. Roman Catholics use the word "infusion" for this act.

In the Sacrament of Baptism, grace eradicates the sin (i.e., original sin) that is found in all humans. Baptism is necessary for salvation. Most are baptized as babies although there is a Rite of Initiation for adults.

In the ritual of Confirmation, a teenager or an adult makes a commitment to Christ as expressed through the Roman Catholic tradition. The candidate is anointed with oil in the shape of a cross on the forehead to signify the presence of the Holy Spirit and they normally add the name of a saint to their name. The zap of grace given in Confirmation is believed by Roman Catholics to give the grace necessary to live a Christian life.

Every important Roman Catholic service includes the *Eucharist* and the most important part of any service is the Eucharist. This explains why Roman Catholics leave a service after the Eucharist, but before the service's finale. It also explains why Roman Catholics are doggedly determined to receive the Eucharist in any given week and on special holy days and why some cities have "Last Chance Eucharists" late on Sunday nights to cover all parishioners.

Especially important is a person's *First Communion*. After a period of instruction, a young elementary school age child is permitted to take communion for the first time. The event is marked by special clothes (white dresses for girls and suits for boys) and celebrations.

Roman Catholics believe that in the consecration of the elements of communion, *Transubstantiation* occurs, a transformation they believe reflects

---

[14] Examples of minor cultural differences include the use of different languages and music.

what Jesus taught in the Bible. Eastern Orthodox believers and some Protestants believe the same idea. Transubstantiation is based on the philosophical distinction between what something actually is (its substance) and what it appears to be (its appearance). In transubstantiation, the bread and wine remain the bread and wine in appearance, but in substance, they become the body and blood of Christ. Roman Catholics base their belief in transubstantiation on John 6:48-59, where Jesus says:

> I am the bread of life. Your forefathers ate manna in the desert, yet they died. But here is the bread that comes down from heaven, which man may eat and not die. I am the living bread that came down from heaven. If anyone eats of this bread, he will live forever. This bread is my flesh which I give for the life of the world. Then the Jews began to grumble among themselves, How can this man give us his flesh to eat? Jesus said to them, I tell you the truth, unless you eat the flesh of the Son of Man and drink his blood, you have no life within you. Whoever eats my flesh and drinks my blood has eternal life, and I will raise him up on the last day. For my flesh is real food, and my blood real drink. Whoever eats my flesh and drinks my blood remains in me and I in him. Just as the living Father sent me and I live because of the Father, so the One who feeds on me will live because of me. This is the bread that came down from heaven. Your forefathers ate manna and died, but he who feeds on this bread will live forever.

Based on these verses, those that believe in transubstantiation teach that believers must eat the body and drink the blood of Jesus to be biblical Christians. They think that those who believe otherwise are simply not following the plain teaching of the Bible.

The Eucharist is given as part of the central act of worship, the *Mass*. There are two parts to the Mass: The Liturgy of the Word and the Liturgy of the Eucharist. During the former, there are Bible readings, prayers, responsive readings, and a sermon, normally called a homily.

The Liturgy of the Eucharist involves the blessing and sharing of the bread and wine. Because the Roman Catholic Church practices closed communion, only Roman Catholics can and should participate. However, there are plenty of instances when non-Roman Catholics participate, even with the full knowledge of the presiding priest.

Communicants come up to the front to receive one or both of the elements. Traditionally, only the bread has been received because in the receiving of one, the blessing of both is conferred. However, in recent years, more and more Roman Catholics take both the bread and the wine.

Another sacrament is Confession or Reconciliation. Penitents confess their sins to a priest and in turn, the priest, in the name of God and representing the God-given institution pronounces forgiveness. Special prayers and other activities may also be required to make amends for the effects of sin.

Prior to Vatican II, Roman Catholics were required to go to a confessional booth prior to receiving the Eucharist. Although this is still available and widely used, other means of face-to-face individual and group confession are also employed.

The fifth sacrament is the Anointing of the Sick (i.e., Extreme Unction or Last Rites). In this ritual, the priest anoints the sick or dying person with oil. This sacrament gives the grace necessary for healing or the grace necessary to face death. In the hit TV show *MASH 4077*, the image of Father Mulcahy giving last rites to dying soldiers during the Korean Conflict is forever imprinted on our minds.[15]

Marriage is the sixth sacrament. Roman Catholics believe that the grace necessary to maintain marriage vows is given during the ritual. This follows a period of required counseling.

The Church teaches that marriage is a lifelong commitment between a man and a woman. It does not recognize same-sex marriage or divorce. A person who divorces and then remarries commits adultery and they cannot receive the sacraments.

However, in special cases the devout may get an *Annulment*, a declaration from the institution that at the time of the marriage, an actual union did not occur. The annulment process is lengthy and can be costly. At times, and in different places, it is easier and cheaper to get.

With an annulment, the faithful can receive the sacraments and remarry with the church's blessing. To the sincere Roman Catholic, the ability to receive grace in the Eucharistic sacrament in particular is crucial. Hence, the annulment is important.

Children resulting from a marriage that is later annulled are considered legitimate and able to receive the sacraments.

The final sacrament is the Ordination of men to the priesthood. This rite gives the individual the grace necessary to be a priest. Only men can be ordained and they must be *Celibate*.[16]

---

[15] *MASH 4077* or *Mobile Army Surgical Unit 4077* traces the antics of a roving medical unit during the Korean War. The show ran from 1972-1983. William Christopher played the unit's chaplain, Father John Patrick Francis Mulcahy for Seasons 1-11 (or Francis John Patrick Mulcahy from Season 8) for the unit.

[16] In recent years in North America, former married Episcopal priests who wish to be ordained as Roman Catholic priests have been allowed to remain married when they convert. The Church has felt that a married priest is better than a divorced one. To do this, the Roman Catholic Church has created the "Pastoral Provision Decision." For an example and more information, see "Married Episcopal Priest will become priest in the Roman Catholic Diocese of Scranton," http://www.freerepublic.com/focus/f-news/1313966/posts

## Institutions

Of all the branches of Christianity, the word *Institution* is most important to Roman Catholics. This is because the Roman Catholic tradition places a great deal of emphasis on the role of the God-established earthly organization in the lives of the faithful. The Church mediates truth and grace through its teachings, sacraments, pronouncements, and priestly structure.

The importance of the institution is also seen at the very beginning of this discussion of Roman Catholicism. Recall that it began with an organizational definition: Roman Catholicism is made up of all the individuals and churches in the world under the authority of the Bishop of Rome. This person is called the *Pope*, the Holy Father, and the Vicar of Christ.

The Pope has power based on an interpretation of Matthew 16:17-19, where Jesus says to the Apostle Peter:

> You are Peter, and upon this rock I will build my church, and the powers of death shall not prevail against it. I will give you the keys of the kingdom of heaven; whatever you bind on earth shall be bound in heaven; whatever you loose on earth shall be loosed in heaven.

The Roman Catholic interpretation of these verses reads: "You are Peter and upon you as Bishop of Rome and upon those who become Bishop after you I will build my church."

This interpretation is based on the tradition that Peter was the first Bishop of Rome. This line of authority traced back to Peter is called apostolic succession. Since Peter, all Popes have been celibate males who served for life and have assumed royal titles on elevation to the papacy.

Even though in the past Popes have assumed power in a variety of ways, honest and dishonest, in recent years, Popes have been elected by the *College of Cardinals* in legitimate, secretive elections. Any real authority that each Pope has tends to be over-emphasized by Protestants (i.e., "Popes are dictators and tell what people have to believe!") and under-emphasized by Roman Catholics (i.e., "I don't have to listen to the Pope to be a devout Roman Catholic.").

One doctrine concerning the Pope confuses non-Roman Catholics: *Papal Infallibility.* Many think that the Church teaches that the Pope is infallible or cannot make wrong choices. For example, if the Pope chooses to go to McDonalds over Burger King, he is infallible. Nothing could be farther from the truth. Papal infallibility means that when the Pope speaks in his official capacity as the head of the church on matters thoroughly discussed by the church, God makes it that he does not speak in error.

The Roman Catholic Church is hierarchical with the Pope at the top assisted by the College of Cardinals and the *Roman Curia.* Serving as advisors, the former handles the election of a new pope. The Curia governs the church. It includes departments such as Church's Congregations, Tribunals and Pontifical Councils.

The church's hierarchical structure includes bishops and archbishops, who direct geographic areas called dioceses. These men appoint local priests with the authority to administer the sacraments.

Faithful men and women can join orders for monks and nuns. Members have to be celibate and they cannot perform the sacraments (unless the males are also ordained as priests). These individuals often serve as full-time religious workers in schools, social service agencies and hospitals.

The core leadership of the worldwide Roman Catholic Church resides in *Vatican City*, an independent enclave in the city of Rome, Italy. Vatican City contains a large library, beautiful art treasures, palaces, and meeting halls. Visibly present is a contingent of Swiss guards dressed in medieval outfits who guard the city. The United States and some other nations have diplomats assigned to represent their nations at the Vatican. For the United States, it is the only diplomat assigned to represent the nation at the headquarters of a religious community.[17]

## SEE WHAT YOU KNOW ABOUT ROMAN CATHOLIC CHRISTIANITY

1. Identify and describe four beliefs.

2. Identify and describe three characteristics of lifestyle.

---

[17] For more information on the Vatican, see http://www.vatican.va/phome_en.htm

3. Identify and describe four characteristics of ceremonies.

4. Identify and describe four characteristics of institutions.

# CHAPTER VI

✠

# INTRODUCTION TO PROTESTANT CHRISTIANITY

This widely diverse branch of the Christian movement has many common features. These will be discussed under the topics "Beliefs and Practices" and "Protestant History" in this chapter.

After these discussions, ensuing chapters will discuss attempts to divide Protestantism into manageable groups to further our understanding of this significant Christian phenomenon.

It is a difficult task to divide today's Protestants into various groups, even though Protestants appear to do a good job separating themselves into different groups. One only has to drive down the street in any city, town, or rural area to see the dizzying number of Protestant groups.

Protestants subdivide because of their stress on individualism (i.e., the lack of a central institution) and the Bible. Protestants gather in groups of like-minded individuals, who find similar beliefs and practices in the Bible.

There are several ways to divide up Protestants, three of which will be discussed in Chapters Seven through Eighteen:

- Divide Protestants by traditionalists and liberals (Chapters Seven through Fourteen)
- Divide Protestants by a three-fold sociological definition: church, sect, and cult (Chapters Fifteen through Seventeen)
- Focus on five groupings by umbrella terms: Anglican/Episcopal, Methodist, Presbyterian/Reformed, Baptist, and Lutheran (Chapter Eighteen)

**Beliefs and Practices**

Protestantism's common beliefs and practices include the following:

- Emphasis on individualism
- The Bible as sole authority
- The right of private interpretation
- Salvation by grace and faith alone
- Protestantism as the gathered fellowship of believers
- The priesthood of all believers
- Protestant ethical diversity
- Protestantism's ceremonial diversity
- Stress on preaching
- Protestant organizational diversity
- Rejection of papal claims in Matthew 16:17-19

At its core, Protestantism emphasizes *Individualism*. This does not mean that Protestants do not associate with one another. Instead, it refers to the belief that each individual can access God without the help of an established institution or hierarchy.[1]

The first and foremost Protestant belief is that the *Bible is the Sole and Central Authority* for what to believe and what to practice. Tradition, which is equal to the Bible in authority for the Eastern Orthodox (tradition up until 1054 CE) and the Roman Catholics (tradition up until this very moment), is supplemental to the Bible. Protestant tradition includes a variety of items, such as the content of preaching and teaching, creeds, hymns, stories of faith, and the Apocrypha. If tradition contradicts what the Bible teaches, tradition is wrong and must be reworked.

Protestants also believe in *the Right of Private Interpretation*. The Bible becomes for the individual Protestant Christian a reference point and a link to God. Thus, they have the ability and the requirement to freely learn and interpret the Bible as they see fit.

Having the Bible as the central authority that each Protestant should freely interpret has been both a blessing and a curse. On one hand, this explains the Protestant stress on Bible study and worldwide Bible translation.

---

[1] This is in direct opposition to the institutionalism of the Roman Catholic tradition from which Protestantism sprung. While Roman Catholics believe that individuals can have a personal connection with God, they stress the role that the church, a God-given institution, plays in their lives. Understanding the importance of individualism to Protestantism and the institutionalism to Roman Catholicism is crucial for helpful religious discussion and dialogue. Too often, debates between these two communities have focused on surface issues, such as the place of saints or a belief in the Pope or purgatory, when the difference lays in approach and emphasis.

After all, if the Bible is the only authority, then everyone should have a Bible and should learn its contents.

On the other hand, it explains why the vast array of Protestant groups exists. Individuals have examined the Bible and have discovered what they believe to be answers to questions about what to believe and how to organize. Then, like-minded believers have formed communities of faiths.

This "chaos of diversity" highlights one of the differences between Protestant individualism and Roman Catholic institutionalism. Roman Catholics argue for the church's role as interpreter of the Bible to prevent this problem.

On the other hand, Protestants respond by saying that God has given each individual the right and ability to access truth in Scripture. Just because people twist the truth does not mean that people as individuals, and not institutions, can access the Bible. According to Protestants, the Roman Catholic tradition has had its cults also.

Protestants believe that *Salvation is a Gift from God and that that Gift comes by Faith alone, not by any Works.* No one is worthy enough to please God. Instead, God sent his Son to die an atoning death to handle the sins of the repentant. This differs from the Eastern Orthodox and Roman Catholic positions that to be "saved," individuals must believe by faith and do good works, such as receiving the sacraments and living a holy life.

As opposed to the institutional focus in Eastern Orthodoxy and Roman Catholicism, Protestantism teaches that the church is made up of *a Gathered Fellowship of Believers.* This is why many Protestant churches say on their church signs that "the so and so church gathers here" or "the so and so church first gathered here on such and such a date."

Finally, Protestants believe in the *Priesthood of all Believers.* This means that instead of having specially chosen people as priests who serve an institution as intermediaries between humans and God, each person is a priest. Because everyone is a priest, each is equally responsible to minister to each other and to non-believers. Protestants believe that some priests are called to be ministers and pastors.

### Protestant Ways of Life

Protestant *Ethical Diversity* is astoundingly broad. However, the Protestant ethical tradition has some common threads.

The most important feature of Protestantism's ethics is the movement's belief in the Bible as the final authority for matters of faith and practice with church tradition serving in only a secondary, supplemental capacity. For the devout, the Bible has the answer for all moral dilemmas, whether by direct command, teaching, or principle. If not clearly laid out, ethical teachings may be inferred from biblical materials.

At its core, Protestantism is best displayed when a single believer does a simple Bible study. The faithful Protestant makes marks in the margins of the

Bible. The Bible, then, functions as a portable church for the individual and provides spiritual sustenance and guidance in the vicissitudes of life. This points to the importance of the individual in Protestantism as opposed to the institution in Roman Catholicism. In Protestantism, the faithful can freely create his/her own ethical system and/or position without an institution's dominating role.

Almost all of Protestantism's ethical systems flow directly from its handling of scripture. This sole source of authority provides the individual believer with an "inspirational ethic": "I feel led by the Holy Spirit to do such and such." This means that no institution, such as the Roman Catholic Magisterium, directs and protects the faithful believer.

The Protestant belief in individual access to scripture is both a "blessing and a curse." On the positive side, Protestants actually study the Bible and apply that study to their individual and corporate religious lives as well as to society as a whole.

On the negative side, a bewildering variety of ethical positions have emerged from Protestants since the Reformation. Roman Catholics, who have continually asked Protestantism as a whole to take stances on ethical issues, have harped on this lack of "speaking with one voice." The absence of a central authoritative institution has lead Roman Catholics to criticize Protestants for their regular creation of new and sometimes cultic movements and ethical systems. Protestants respond that God speaks directly to them and that they have checks and balances (i.e., other like-minded individual believers). Moreover, just because a person creates some questionable ethical systems does not alter the fundamental issue that individuals should be able to create ethics for themselves through Bible study.

Protestantism's belief in the Bible as final authority may be simply stated, but its implementation is not. The real issue is biblical interpretation. Some Protestants say that anything may or may not be done if the Bible does not clearly forbid an action by direct command or inference. Others believe that nothing can be done unless the Bible specifically commands it.

Another division found among Protestants is between traditionalists and modernists. The former sees eternal unchanging truths or commands in scripture that never change despite changing culture. The latter say that some of the truths held to be eternal were, in fact, part of a time and place. These should be dropped and other trans-historical truths should be emphasized.[2]

Another core belief of Protestantism is that an individual is saved by grace through faith alone. God freely forgives human beings through the sacrifice of his Son rather than by works. Human beings cannot and should not do anything to merit God's forgiveness.

Protestantism's stress on salvation by grace through faith alone impacts the Protestant view of Natural Law, which is so important for Roman Catho-

---

[2] See Chapters Seven and Fourteen.

lic ethics. To Protestantism, Natural Law suggests that humans have the ability to act morally on their own. This is anathema to Protestantism. As a result, the Natural Law argument is missing from Protestant arguments.

Due to varying interpretations, Protestants differ on the interplay of predestination and free will (or another version, "once saved, always saved" or "once damned always damned"). This has implications for ethics.

Some of those in the former camp have argued that living an ethical life is unimportant because the saved will be saved anyway. This contributes to a de-emphasis on human responsibility for morals and ethical actions. It might be said that "God made me do it" or "The Devil made me do it." Another cadre in the predestination group believes that those predestined for heaven will demonstrate that fact through moral lives as individuals and societies.

Those Protestants who stress human free will with the potential loss of salvation, emphasize the role of the individual in developing and maintaining a moral life. Living the ethical life is crucial because the saved might not keep salvation. They might say, "I made me do it."

Protestant belief in the priesthood of all believers impacts ethics; all believers have a shared responsibility for faithful living as individuals and as members in the religious community. Faithful living involves the larger social context as well. Out of this priesthood, some become ministers. This bottom-up mentality replaces the Roman Catholic top-down hierarchical system with specially designated priests who represent the institution.

### Ceremonies

It is no surprise that Protestants have an astounding amount of *Ceremonial Diversity*. They disagree on many aspects of ritual life, such as the number, meaning, and carrying out of core rituals.

Although 99% of all Protestants agree that Jesus commanded his followers to practice at least two central rituals (baptism and communion), they disagree that there are only two. While most believe in just two, some Protestants add up to seven. These additions may or may not mirror those practiced by Roman Catholics or Eastern Christians. Uniquely Protestant core rituals include foot washing and a holy kiss.

A few Protestant groups or movements with Protestant origins maintain that there are no rituals or at least no physical rituals commanded (i.e., the Salvation Army, the Christian Science Church, and Quakerism).

Protestants differ on whether they call these two rituals ordinances or sacraments. These terms are used to separate views about when and how God's grace is received by the devout. An ordinance is carried out in remembrance of grace (God's saving power) already received. It is a testimony of the prior experience of God's grace. In a sacrament, the individual receives a zap of God's grace in the ritual itself.

Among Protestants there is a wide variety of ways by which these rituals occur. For example, Protestants either baptize infants or wait until they are old enough to accept Christ for themselves prior to baptism. They use water to immerse, sprinkle, or make a mark on the baptizee's forehead. Baptisms occur in creeks or in tanks or in fonts inside churches. Officially ordained or lay people carry out the ritual.

The sharing of bread and wine in remembrance of Christ's death is called a variety of terms by Protestants, ranging from the Eucharist to Holy Communion or the Lord's Supper. Bread and wine may be used, but also crackers and grape juice or crackers and water. Some Protestants go down to the front of the church to receive Communion, while others sit in their seats as the elements are passed around. Many Protestants drink from a common cup, while others have his or her own cup. Officially ordained or lay people may direct the ritual.

All Protestants deny that Christ is somehow re-sacrificed each time communion takes place as Roman Catholicism teaches. However, they have a variety of views about the meaning of what transpires spiritually in the ritual itself.[3]

It is no surprise that *Preaching* has central importance to Protestantism. Because Protestants believe that the Bible is the sole and central authority for faith and practice, the Bible should be taught and learned. For most Protestant worshippers, the preaching of the Word is the most important aspect of worship. Often when they leave church, they say to each other, "What did you think of the sermon?" This is opposite of Roman Catholicism and Eastern Orthodoxy, where the focus is on receiving the Eucharist and the sermon or homily is so short as to be often forgotten. More often, a Roman Catholic can miss the sermon and receive the sacrament and still feel fulfilled.

A Protestant is just the opposite. Protestants stress the importance of homiletics (preaching) to their would-be pastors. Most Protestants, by reputation, produce good preachers. Protestant Church architecture often reflects the importance of the Bible as opposed to the importance of communion. This emphasis on the teaching of the Bible is seen in church services and church architecture. A local church's central piece of architecture is its pulpit, which stands out prominently, often on a raised platform. The communion table often stands beneath the pulpit on the main floor and is often less ornate.

### Organizations

It is no surprise that Protestants have *Organizational Diversity*. Each Protestant group feels that the Bible teaches different ways of organizing and Protestants are organized in three ways:

- Congregational
- Connectional
- Hierarchical style

---

[3] See Chapters Six and Eight through Eighteen.

Protestants may or may not be attached to local, regional, national, and international religious organizations of like-minded individuals.

Some Protestants call their groups *Community Churches*. This term is supposed to be a reference to totally independent churches based in a local area. While this is true for many groups, some community churches are really part of larger groups, which may have any one of the three governmental styles. These have chosen not to identify themselves as having a certain religious affiliation as a way to attract un-churched people, who would rather join a community rather than denominational church.

Protestants (and their Eastern Christian counterparts) *Reject the Roman Catholic Interpretation of Matthew 16:17-19*. Instead, they believe that when Jesus said to Peter, "You are Peter and upon this rock, I will build my church," he defined rock as Peter's faith, not Peter himself and his successors. Jesus said, "I will build my church on those that have faith like Peter."

### Protestant History

Protestants have a shared history. They all trace their roots to religious movements that emerged in Western Christianity between the 1300s and the 1600s CE. This time period is called "The Reformations" because there were, in actuality, two self-contained but interacting Reformations: the Protestant Reformation and the Roman Catholic Reformation.[4]

The Protestant Reformation had four founding movements, each similar and yet each different:

- Anglican
- Calvinist
- Anabaptist
- Lutheran

These four movements were similar in that each had common Protestant features and each was different with distinctive traits. All Protestant groups

---

[4] The Roman Catholic Church began using the term "Counter-Reformation" in the 19th century CE to describe the church's response to the Protestant Reformation in the 16th and 17th centuries CE. However, the term Counter-Reformation is too limiting a term. A genuine period of revival and reform occurred within the Roman-dominated Western church, which constructed a tradition, which lasted until Vatican II. This tradition included a more efficient central government, a renewed liturgy and a clearer statement of beliefs (i.e., transubstantiation, purgatory, veneration of saints and the sale of indulgences). Post-Trent Roman Catholicism had a vigor and self-exuberance, which exhibited itself in church architecture, decoration, art, music, ritual, a new style of devotional literature (i.e., Francis de Sales, *Introduction to the Devout Life*), and fervent missionary zeal both inside and outside Roman Catholic Europe.

have emerged either directly or as combinations of two or more groups (i.e., modern-day Lutheranism directs its heritage directly back to Martin Luther, modern-day Methodism began in an Anglican context and modern-day Baptists are a combination of all four, even though they could be misconstrued to be a direct derivative of the Anabaptists). An outline of the four movements follows.

### The Anglican

The Anglican Reformation was the Reformation found in England. The term Anglican is derived from the Latin phrase "Anglicana Ecclesia," literally, the English church.

English Christianity began long before the infamous stories of *Henry VIII* (1491-1547 CE) and his many wives. Prior to Henry, this branch of Christianity had two forms, *Celtic* and Roman, with the latter winning ascendancy at the Synod of Whitby (663/664 CE).[5] Until Henry VIII, Roman Catholic Christianity maintained its dominance.

The event that triggered the Anglican Reformation was secular in nature and was part of the English desire to be independent from continental Europe religiously and politically.

Wanting a male heir, Henry VIII needed to divorce Catherine of Aragon. When the Pope turned down his request, Henry and the English Parliament declared him the "Supreme Head on Earth of the Church of England," thereby renouncing the authority of the Pope on English soil. All financial, judicial, and administrative connections were severed and many monasteries were taken over by the state. Despite these changes, Henry VIII's English church retained Roman views on many things, such as the sacraments and salvation by grace and works.

Henry VIII's son, Edward VI (1547-1553 CE), led the church along more Protestant lines in liturgy and doctrine as evidenced by the Prayer Books of 1549 and 1552 CE. After his death, Mary Tudor (1553-1558 CE) tried to remake England into a Roman Catholic state. During this time many of Edward's reformers were martyred, hence the name Bloody Mary. These included: Thomas Cranmer, Nicholas Ridley, and Hugh Latimer as well as many ordinary people. Elizabeth I (1558-1603 CE) restored Protestantism to Eng-

---

[5] Little is known about the introduction of Christianity into Britain. A longtime tradition states that Joseph of Arimathea introduced the Christian faith soon after the death of Jesus. By the 4th century CE, British Christianity was sufficiently organized to send delegates to church councils (i.e., Arles, 314, and Arminum, 359 CE).

Celtic Christianity consisted of a network of remote, independent monasteries headed by powerful abbots. It was known for its missionary zeal, scholarship, rich artistic tradition, and asceticism. Today, there is a resurgence of interest in Celtic Christianity. See Ian Bradley, *Celtic Christianity: Making Myths and Chasing Dreams* (Edinburgh: Edinburgh University Press, 2005 reprint).

land through the Elizabethan Settlement, which established a comprehensive, national, Episcopal church with the monarch as Supreme Governor. This created a church with a close church-state relationship. The Pope had no authority. The church retained a sacramental theology based on two rituals, baptism and communion.

### The Calvinist

This branch of the Protestant Reformation is named after *John Calvin* (1509-1564 CE). Calvin was a Frenchman, with an extensive educational background in scholasticism and humanism. After his religious conversion, he left his native France for areas of European where the reforming spirit of Protestantism dominated.[6]

After a brief stint in Geneva and then some travels in Europe, Calvin returned to Geneva by invitation in 1541 CE. From then on, he never held any elective or official office. Nevertheless, Calvin and his ideas had an enormous impact on the city. Education and public welfare were drastically improved. The reform of the Genevan church was accomplished largely through the *Ecclesiastical Ordinances* (1541).

Calvin was a diligent correspondent, fervent preacher with an intense pastoral concern, and most important, a theologian. As opposed to Luther, the impassioned preacher, Calvin was the Protestant Reformation's first great theologian, its first great systematizer of thought. In 1536 CE, he wrote the first edition of his theological treatise, *Institutes of the Christian Religion.*

Calvin's place in history rests on his theology, as expressed by his actions (in Geneva) and his writings.[7]

Calvin's ideas were marked by extensions of Luther's thoughts with his own particular twists and turns. Calvin believed in Luther's onlys (the Bible, faith, and Christ's grace alone).

Calvin's biblical interpretation was different than Luther in at least one arena. He stated that if the Bible did not teach a practice or belief, it could not be done. So as opposed to Lutheran-influenced churches, Calvinist-influenced churches generally have been a lot simpler, lacking candles, stained glass windows, and clergy in fancy robes. Calvin emphasized the sovereignty of God in all human life, which led to the doctrine of *Predestination* (i.e., God foreknows and predetermines the outcome of all things).

Calvin believed that Christians should live moral lives and should try to transform society because this is a way to be an obedient Christian.

---

[6] "God by a sudden conversion subdued and brought my mind to a teachable frame, which was more hardened in such matters than might have been expected from one at my early period of life." See John Calvin, "Preface," *Commentary on the Book of Psalms* 1, trans. James Anderson (Grand Rapids: Eerdmans, 1948), p. XL.

[7] These include his biblical commentaries and successive editions of the *Institutes* with definitive editions in 1559 and 1560 CE.

For Calvin, a church is a place where the Word of God is preached in a pure form and heard and the sacraments carried out according to the institution of Christ.[8] The sacraments are baptism and communion.

Calvin believed that churches should be run by teaching and ruling *Elders*, not bishops. These elders met on local and broader geographic levels. He taught that church and state should be closely linked with separate responsibilities. As portrayed in Nathaniel Hawthorne's *Scarlet Letter*, the church pronounces adultery as sin and the state carries out the prescribed punishment for the sin.

The Calvinist Reformation could be found in Switzerland, the Low Countries, England, Scotland, and later the United States, in Presbyterianism and Puritanism.

### The Anabaptist

This branch of the Protestant Reformation has often been called the *Radical* or *Left Wing Reformation* because of the movement's rejection of some major tenets of the other Reformation groups and the Roman Catholic Church, including the close link of church and state and infant baptism.

The Anabaptist Movement had a vast array of characters and locations. Because they appeared wherever persecution did not touch them, no particular geographic area was associated with them. The Anabaptists settled in the Low Countries, Great Britain, Scotland, and North America. However, the original movement began in Zurich in 1523 CE when the Reformation triggered questions about church rituals, in particular, baptism. *Conrad Grebel* (1498-1526 CE) and *Felix Manz* (1498-1527 CE) preached and baptized adults in the area, even if they had been already baptized as infants.

By 1526 CE, the fledgling movement had begun to suffer persecution. Manz was drowned to mimic believers' baptism and many others were martyred. Many were exiled. Those who remained went underground.

Anabaptists could be found in Switzerland under the leadership of Conrad Grebel and Felix Manz, in southern Germany under Balthasar Hubmaier and Hans Denck, in Moravia with the Hutterites, and in the Netherlands and northern Germany with the Mennonites.

Anabaptists believed in the primacy of Scripture. They rejected infant baptism because they argued that a person had to be old enough to believe for themselves prior to baptism. Because of this belief, Anabaptists insisted that those baptized as infants had to be re-baptized (Hence, the term *Anabaptist*, which means to re-baptize).

Anabaptists believed in strict church discipline and the creation of a pure believer's church. They had deep moral earnestness and sought to model their lives after Christ. Anabaptists were pacifists and refused to swear oaths.

---

[8] John Calvin, *Institutes of the Christian Religion*, revised ed., 4.1.9 (Peabody: Hendrickson Publishers, 2008).

Anabaptists believed in the total *Separation of Church and State*. They distrusted the state and other churches because of intense persecution. Martyrdom became the norm in Anabaptist circles and to this day, many have *The Martyrs Mirror* and the Bible on their nightstands to remind them of what their predecessors endured.[9]

### The Lutheran

The Lutheran movement is most closely linked to Germany, Scandinavia, and later the United States. This part of Protestantism was launched by *Martin Luther* (1483-1546 CE). He is remembered as the "impassioned preacher and pastor" of the Protestant Reformation.

Luther was born in Eisleben, a copper miner's son, and educated on the university level at Erfurt. In July 1505 CE, he entered an Augustinian monastery after he had made a vow to God in a "moment of terror" when he was thrown from his horse during a thunderstorm. Luther was ordained in 1507 CE as a Roman Catholic priest. In 1512 CE, he received a Doctor of Theology degree and became professor of scripture at the University of Wittenberg.

During his professorship, Luther became increasingly troubled by his own personal guilt before God and pastorally concerned about the Western church's trafficking in indulgences.[10] He protested with his famous *95 Theses*. This began a controversy that lasted the rest of his lifetime and triggered the German Reformation. In 1520 CE, the Pope excommunicated Luther (*Exsurge Domine*, which stated his teachings were heretical and the *Decet Romanum Pontificem*, which officially excommunicated Luther). Luther was summoned to appear before Charles V at an Imperial Diet at Worms in 1521 CE, where Luther refused to recant his views unless persuaded by the Bible.

For a period, Luther was under the protection of the Elector of Saxony. He worked on his translation of the New Testament into German, as well as several devotional books. Luther spent much of his time in private and public debates with Roman Catholics and other Protestant leaders. He supported the German nobility in opposition to the German peasantry, although he called on the nobility to treat the peasantry well.

In 1525 CE, Luther married an ex-nun, Catherine von Bora. He faced constant controversy, intermittent poor health (i.e., bubonic plague), be-

---

[9] Thieleman J. van Bragt authored this book in Dutch in 1660 CE. It has a rather long and descriptive title: *The Bloody Theater or Martyrs Mirror of the Defenseless Christians who baptized only upon confession of faith, and who suffered and died for the testimony of Jesus, their Saviour, from the time of Christ to the year A.D. 1660*. The *Martyrs Mirror* documents the stories and testimonies of Christian martyrs from the age of the apostles until the time of the Anabaptists. This book is especially important for contemporary Amish and Mennonite believers.

[10] The Roman Catholic Church sold indulgences to finance the building of St. Peter's Basilica in Rome, Italy. The purchased indulgence provided the means for a soul to leave purgatory and journey to heaven.

reavement, and the loss of colleagues through intense persecution. Despite these things, he was a genuinely pastoral man and his home offered hospitality to a steady stream of visitors. Luther may have most often been found at the local pub where he would drink beer and debate fine points of theology with deep pastoral concerns among friend and foe.

The controversy that Luther launched was created by many of his ideas, which could be found in many of his famous works. Luther was an author, especially in 1520 CE when he produced some of his most famous works (*On Good Works*, *The Babylonian Captivity of the Church*, *Address to the German Nobility*, and *The Freedom of the Christian*).

Partially because of his writings, Luther's central ideas later found their way into the other branches of the Protestant Reformation. Luther began the Protestant stress on "onlys" or "alones":

| | |
|---|---|
| • Scripture alone <br> *Sola Scriptura*:: | Scripture alone is the ultimate basis for what to believe and practice, not scripture and tradition. |
| • Faith Alone <br> *Sola Fide*: | Salvation comes through personal faith, not through a combination of personal faith and human works. |
| • Grace Alone <br> *Sola Gratia*: | Salvation is not earned, but is freely given through God's grace. |

Luther's sola scriptura included a particular approach to biblical interpretation: Luther taught that if the Bible did not forbid an action or thought, it was up to the individual believer to make a choice whether to do or think it.

This idea had a very practical impact. Lutheran churches to this day have stained glass windows, candles on fancy altars and ministers with colorful robes. They (and Luther) would say, "Where in the Bible does it forbid these things?" Since it does not, Lutherans have chosen to have them.

Luther asserted the priesthood of all believers. This means that instead of having specially chosen people as priests who serve an institution as intermediaries between humans and God, each person is a priest. Because everyone is a priest, each is equally responsible to minister to each other and to non-believers. Protestants believe that some priests are called to be ministers and pastors.

Luther's view of marriage typified what would later become accepted Protestant practice: Clergy may marry and live normal human lives. Clergy do not remain celibate and live outside the main realm of human activity.

Luther believed that individuals should live moral lives in grateful response to what Christ did for them by his death.

Advocating his *Two-Kingdom Theory*, Luther believed a close connection of church and state with each having set functions in society. The spiritual kingdom (i.e., the church) is made up of individuals who have experienced God's grace and who operate with faith and love. The earthly kingdom (i.e., secular governments) operates by the law through the sword and compulsion with the goal of maintaining order and peace.

**SEE WHAT YOU KNOW ABOUT THE INTRODUCTION TO PROTESTANTISM**

1. Identify and describe four beliefs.

2. Identify and describe three characteristics of lifestyle.

3. Identify and describe four characteristics of ceremonies.

4. Identify and describe three characteristics of institutions.

# CHAPTER VII
## ✠
# TRADITIONAL AND LIBERAL PROTESTANTISM

The first way to divide Protestants is by *Traditional* or *Liberal* (i.e., Modernist). Traditionalists and modernists may be found in their own Protestant groups or they may be found in the same community of faith. The presence of traditionalists and liberals in the same Protestant group has been a major flash point in large Protestant denominations in recent years over approaches to scripture and ethics (i.e., the place of homosexuals and the roles of women).

Chapter Seven introduces the traditional and liberal division of Protestantism. Chapters Nine through Fourteen describe a variety of traditional and liberal groups.

Traditionalists and modernists divide over how to see and read the Bible. Different ways of understanding the following questions divide these two groups:

- What is the origin of the Bible?
- Who selected the Bible's books? What reasons were used?
- Is the Bible accurate?
- What authority does the Bible possess?
- Does the Bible have unity of thought?
- What is the purpose of the Bible?
- When it comes to biblical interpretation, what is the relationship between the Bible and contemporary culture?

### On the Origin of the Bible
Traditionalists:
God inspired authors to write the books found in the Bible.

Modernists:
Human authors wrote the books found in the Bible.

### On the Selection of Books found in the Bible
Traditionalists:
Both Jews and Christians believe that God led them to choose which books belonged in their collections. For example, Christian leaders under the guidance of the Holy Spirit by the 4th century CE affirmed what had been already taken for granted: certain inspired New Testament books were accepted and others were rejected. Those included were inerrant or free from error. Three criteria marked book selection: apostolic authorship, widespread use, and agreement with apostolic teaching.

Modernists:
Humans collaborated to choose which books should be included in the Bible. For example, church leaders selected those New Testament books that mirrored their beliefs. They purposely rejected those that promoted the movements within Christianity that they did not accept as authentic versions of the Truth (Gnostic and Jewish Christianity). Was it a human plot that thwarted God's will, which has only now come light? See Dan Brown's *The Da Vinci Code*.[1]

### On the Accuracy of the Bible
Traditionalists:
The Bible is accurate because God inspired the authors of the Bible to write texts that were errorless. Although there are no original texts (i.e., autographs) of any biblical book, there are accurate copies and an accurate established text for the Old and New Testaments. It is a mistake to assume that copies of originals are not accurate. The Bible is correct when it describes religious faith and practice only (limited inerrancy) or in anything it describes (total inerrancy). While minor copying errors have crept into the texts over the centuries, these have no impact on significant religious beliefs. Apparent contradictions appear in the Bible. But, these can be harmonized with little thought, a few can be attributed to copying errors and those that cannot be understood will be one day when full truth is known. Most Bible translations are reliable. This is particularly true for the *New International Version*.

Modernists:
The Bible is an inaccurate document written by spiritually aware, but fallible authors. There are no originals (i.e., autographs) of any Bible

---

[1] Dan Brown, *The Da Vinci Code*, 1st ed. (New York: Doubleday, 2003). For a good analysis of this approach, see Philip Jenkins, *Hidden Gospels: How the Church Lost its Way* (New York: Oxford University Press, 2002).

book. However, scholars have established a valid text for both the Old and New Testaments. Still, these have all sorts of contradictions which cannot be resolved. There is very little historicity in the Bible. Jesus actually said only a few of the words attributed to him and the findings of contemporary science have shown that the Bible is inaccurate (i.e., creation, demons causing mental illness, etc.).

### On the Authority of the Bible
Traditionalists:

The Bible has divine authority derived from its status as a God-inspired text and because it is God's will. The Bible has authority when discussing religious concerns only (limited inerrancy) or all concerns (full inerrancy).

Modernists:

The Bible is a human book without any authority beyond humanity. It contains God's will, but it is not God's will.

### On the Bible's Unity of Thought
Traditionalists:

The Bible is unified thematically, which is quite remarkable. It is the story of God and his interaction with creation, especially humans, through a series of covenants.

Modernists:

The Bible lacks unified thought. Instead, it reflects the opinions of its writers over 1,500 years in a variety of contexts and from a variety of presuppositions.

### On the Bible's Purpose
Traditionalists:

The Bible's purpose is to communicate God's will to humanity so that individuals can live in accordance with God's will.

Modernists:

The Bible's purpose is to tell the religious stories of a variety of individuals to inspire its readers to live in accordance with God's will.

### On the Relationship between the Bible and Contemporary Culture
Traditionalists:

Although culture can impact the writing and meaning of texts, the Bible's teachings transcend time and place. The Bible contains eternal, unchanging truths, which remain constant despite changing culture. For example, since the Bible says that homosexuality is wrong, it is wrong even though contemporary culture is more accepting of the gay lifestyle.

Modernists:

Because many Bible passages are limited by time and culture, some parts are not suitable guides for today (i.e., passages dealing with slavery, ordering genocide, rejecting homosexuality, and restricting roles for women). Instead other biblical eternal truths should be emphasized, which seem to reflect current culture, such as tolerance, acceptance and love. For example, since many in the modern world have come to accept homosexuality, the Bible's teachings against such activity should be ignored.

### SEE WHAT YOU KNOW ABOUT TRADITIONAL AND LIBERAL PROTESTANTS

1. Describe how Traditional and Liberal Protestants differ on the origin of the Bible.

2. Describe how Traditional and Liberal Protestants differ on how the books of the Bible were selected.

3. Describe how Traditional and Liberal Protestants differ on the accuracy of the Bible.

4. Describe how Traditional and Liberal Protestants differ on the authority of the Bible.

5. Describe how Traditional and Liberal Protestants differ on the Bible's unity of thought.

6. Describe how Traditional and Liberal Protestants differ on the purpose of the Bible.

7. Describe how Traditional and Liberal Protestants differ on the relationship of the Bible and contemporary culture.

CHAPTER VIII

✠

TRADITIONALISTS AND LIBERALS IN THE
SAME MOVEMENT:
THE EMERGING CHURCH AND
STONE-CAMPBELL RESTORATIONISM

*Emerging Church*[1]
The first example of traditionalists and liberals found in the same Protestant
movement is the Emerging Church. Adherents call this movement a "conversation" rather than a church because it suggests an evolving dialogue.
Although the movement eschews labels as too defining, supporters can be
"evangelical," "post-evangelical," "liberal," "post-liberal," "conservative"
and/or "post-conservative."

The term "Emerging Church" is used for a Christian movement that
hunts for ties with *Post-modern* people, particularly the un-churched. This late
20th and early 21st century CE group claims to have a mixture of theological
traditionalists and liberals and it is particularly active in North America,
Western Europe, Australia, New Zealand, and Africa. Since the 1980s CE, it

---

[1] Pivotal books on the Emerging Church include: Eddie Gibbs and Ryan K. Bolger,
*Emerging Churches: Creating Christian Community in Post Modern Cultures* (Grand Rapids:
Baker Book House, 2005); Doug Pagitt, *Church Re-imagined: The Spiritual Formation of
People in Communities of Faith* (Grand Rapids: Zondervan, 2005); Steve Taylor, *The Out
of Bounds Church?: Learning to Create a Church in a Culture of Change* (Grand Rapids:
Zondervan, 2005); Michael Frost and Alan Hirsch, *The Shaping of Things to Come: Innovation and Mission for the 21ˢᵗ Century Church* (Peabody: Hendrickson Publishing, 2003);
and Brian McLaren, *A New Kind of Christian: A Tale of Two Friends on a Spiritual Journey*
(San Francisco: Jossey-Bass, 2001). Important websites on Emerging Churches include: ZoeCarnate.com, The Ooze.com, Acts29network.com, leadnet.com, emer-
gentvillage.com and Synagague3000.org (for Jews).

has become a large grassroots movement among clergy and laity in mainline Protestant churches. Emergents also attend local independent churches or house churches.

The most public face of the Emerging Church Movement is *Rev. Brian McLaren*, a prolific author, speaker, and organizer.[2]

Common emphases found among emerging believers include a mission to make Christianity relevant, dissatisfaction with traditional churches and theological expressions and methods, and a willingness to engage contemporary culture, which is seen as post-modern.

To implement these ideas, supporters emphasize several things. First, they believe that the Bible's value can be found in how it "speaks to individual and group stories" rather than in its propositional truths. This point that the Bible is not propositional is supported by this McLaren quote, "This rebuke to the arrogant, intellectualizing is especially apt for modern Christians, who do not build cathedrals of stone and glass as in the Middle Ages, but rather conceptual cathedrals." Instead he emphasizes the "mystical/poetic" approach to the scriptures and says, "the Bible itself contains precious little expository prose."[3]

Next, Emerging believers encourage a variety of biblical interpretations. They claim that they are creating protected surroundings for opinions typically rejected by Evangelicalism and Fundamentalism. An example of this is what McLaren says about hell: "In the Bible, save means rescue or heal. It emphatically does not mean save from hell or give eternal life after death as many preachers seem to imply . . . In general, in any context, save means get out of trouble. The trouble could be sickness, war, political intrigue, oppressions, poverty, imprisonment or any kind of danger or evil."[4]

---

[2] Some of McLaren's bestselling books include: *The Church on the Other Side: Doing Ministry in the Postmodern Matrix* (Grand Rapids: Zondervan, 1998, rev. ed. 2000); *Finding Faith* (Grand Rapids: Zondervan, 1999): *A New Kind of Christian* (San Francisco: Jossey-Bass/Leadership Network, 2001); *More Ready Than You Realize: Evangelism as Dance in the Postmodern Matrix* (Grand Rapids: Zondervan, 2002); Coauthored with Leonard Sweet, *A is for Abductive* (Grand Rapids: Zondervan, 2002); Coauthored with Anthony Campolo, *Adventures in Missing the Point: How the Culture-Controlled Church Neutered the Gospel* (Grand Rapids: Zondervan/Youth Specialties, 2006); *The Story We Find Ourselves In* (San Francisco: Jossey-Bass, 2003); *A Generous Orthodoxy* (Grand Rapids: Zondervan/Youth Specialties, 2006); and *The Secret Message of Jesus: Uncovering the Truth that Could Change Everything* (Nashville: Thomas Nelson, 2006). McLaren's international stature was demonstrated in July 2008 CE when he, a non-Anglican/Episcopalian, made a presentation on emerging church themes as applied to Anglicanism to the most recent Lambeth Conference at the behest of the Archbishop of Canterbury.
[3] McLaren, *A Generous Orthodoxy*, p. 155.
[4] McLaren, *A Generous Orthodoxy*, p. 93.

Third, advocates believe that it is necessary to "deconstruct" traditional Christian dogma and avoid the use of "christianize," a jargon that is not understandable to modern culture.

Also, non-critical interfaith dialogue and evangelism by example are encouraged in place of what Emergents feel has been the use of aggressive evangelistic techniques.

Fifth, most Emergents do not adhere to the social positions of Evangelicalism and Fundamentalism, such as abstaining from alcohol, using profanity and watching movies with explicit sexual content. They wish to expand ethics beyond pietistic individualism and add themes of social justice and environmentalism. This holistic involvement takes many forms, such as social activism, hospitality, and acts of kindness. They call this *Missional Living*.

An example of this approach to ethics can be found in Emergent views on homosexuality. McLaren has said:

Frankly, many of us don't know what we should think about homosexuality. We've heard all sides but no position has yet won our confidence. . . We know that the biblical arguments are nuanced and multilayered, and the pastoral ramifications are staggeringly complex. We aren't sure if or where lines are to be drawn, nor do we know how to enforce with fairness whatever lines are drawn.[5]

Finally, Emergents use the Internet to communicate via blogs, websites, and on-line videos and take elements of worship from a wide range of Christian traditions, such as Anglicanism, Roman Catholicism, Eastern and Celtic Christianities. They may use liturgy, prayer beads, icons, spiritual directors, and the *Lectio Divina*.[6] Some Emergent communities are neo-charismatic and use contemporary Christian music.

---

[5] http://blog.christianitytoday.com/outofur/archives/2006/01/brian_mclaren_ o_ 2.html

[6] Lectio Divina is Latin for "divine reading." It may also be called "holy reading" or "spiritual reading." It refers to the daily Christian practice of scripture reading and prayer with the purpose of developing a relationship with God. Normally practiced for one hour, it consists of four parts: Lectio (a slow reading of the Bible passage), Meditatio (focusing on a passage or words in a passage), Oratio (an intuitive dialogue or conversation with God), and Contemplatio (a moment of pure contemplation of God). This was first suggested around 1150 CE by Guigo II, the ninth prior of Grande Chartreuse, in his book called *Scala Claustralium* or *The Monk's Ladder*. This book includes a four step process of scripture reading and prayer: reading, meditation, prayer, and contemplation.

### Stone-Campbell Restorationism

A second example of traditionalists and modernists in the same movement can be found in the churches of Restorationism that are not part of the Joseph Smith tradition (see Chapter Sixteen):

- Churches of Christ with approximately 1.5 million members in the United States
- Independent Christian Churches/Churches of Christ with approximately 700,000 members in the United States
- The Christian Church (Disciples of Christ) with approximately 723,000 members in the United States.[7]

The first and second are traditionalist, while the third has a mixture of traditionalists and liberals.

### Background

In the wake of the early 19th century CE revivals in the United States with leaders such as *Barton Stone* and *Thomas and Alexander Campbell,* many people became increasingly dismayed over the diversity of Protestant religious groups in North America. They asked, "Why are there all these divisions?," "Is there one true church?," "If there is one true church, what should it believe and practice?"

Added to these, was a sense that the church as it existed in the early 1800s CE lacked the vibrant piety found in the New Testament church. "Is there one church that believes and practices real New Testament Christianity?"

Stone and the Campbells launched movements which would merge in 1832 CE with the name, Christian, given to Stone's followers and Disciples of Christ given to the followers of the Campbells. Names were given that could be found in the Bible because Restorationists believed it was inappropriate and divisive to name churches after people or places, such as Luther or Anglican.

In ensuing years, the movement split into three groups—the Churches of Christ, the Independent Christian Church/Churches of Christ, and the Christian Church (Disciples of Christ).[8]

---

[7] For statistics on for statistics on the Churches of Christ, see *Churches of Christ in the United States* (Nashville: 21st Century Christian, 2006).

For statistics on the Independent Christian Churches/Churches of Christ, see *Directory of the Ministry* at http://www.directoryoftheministry.com/

For the Christian Church (the Disciples of Christ), see Sharon E. Watkins, *Yearbook & Directory of the Christian Church (Disciples of Christ)* [Indianapolis: The Office of The General Minister and President, 2006].

See also Douglas Allen Foster and Anthony L. Dunnavant, *The Encyclopedia of the Stone-Campbell Movement: Christian Church (Disciples of Christ), Christian Churches/Churches of Christ, Churches of Christ* (Grand Rapids: Wm. B. Eerdmans Publishing, 2004).

See Chapter Sixteen for a discussion of Joseph Smith Restorationism.

Restorationists believe that it was Christ's goal to establish one united church. They wish to see Christ's prayer that all his followers be one is fulfilled (John 17:21). Disunity is evidenced by human-created religious institutions, theologies, and creeds.

Restorationists believe that the way to create authentic Christianity is to make a radical turn back to the New Testament church where a pattern exists to copy. In their attempt to establish churches based on their understanding of the New Testament, Restorationists teach that the Bible is the sole authority for faith and practice. They say, "No creed but the Bible; We are to be Christians only; Where scriptures speak, we speak, where scriptures are silent, we are silent."[9]

However, these Christians do agree on how to interpret "where scriptures are silent." Some believe that the Bible must clearly command something or at least establish a belief or practice via inference for something to be obeyed. For example, if a word like "Trinity" does not appear in the Bible, it should not be used (i.e., some Restorationists use the term Godhead instead of Trinity).

Other Restorationists argue that things unmentioned in the Bible fall into the category of opinion. Hence, it becomes a matter of local congregational or individual choice what is believed or practiced in a particular area. For example, some of these Restorationists accept the use of instrumental music in worship because it falls under the category of opinion.

The movement also believed that the New Testament pattern taught that each person has total free choice to accept or reject the Gospel. There is no original sin. Each church should be self-governing bodies with regular non-liturgical services. The Lord's Supper as a memorial should be served at each meeting of the church and individuals should be baptized by full immersion.

### The Churches of Christ

The Churches of Christ is the largest Restorationist group. The Bible, in particular the New Testament, is the sole authority for matters of faith and practice. Creeds, theologies and denominations are human creations and none are bases for belief and actions.

In matters of faith and practice, members seek "to speak where the Bible speaks and to be silent where the Bible is silent." To these churches, actions and beliefs can only be accepted if they are found in the Bible, either by direct statements or inference.

---

[8] The 1906 United States Census listed the Disciples of Christ and the Churches of Christ as separate groups. The 1971 *Yearbook of American Churches* has the Independent Christian Churches/Churches of Christ as separate institutions from the Disciples of Christ.

[9] http://www.bibletruths.net/Archives/BTAR106.htm

Humans have free will and no original sin. Salvation comes through obedience to the facts of the Gospel at and after the age of accountability
(around age 13). The steps to salvation are:

- A person needs to be taught
- A person needs to believe
- A person needs to repent
- A person needs to confess
- A person needs to be baptized by immersion
- A person needs to remain faithful

The Church believes that for a person to be truly saved, they repent of
their sins, confess Christ and be immediately baptized in that local church. If
the last step is never taken, a person's salvation is questioned. For this reason,
baptism generally occurs immediately after a person accepts Christ as Lord
and Savior. Only those who have been properly baptized are true Christians.
Salvation can be lost if a person does not remain faithful.

The Churches of Christ are non-liturgical, have weekly communion and
sing *A Cappella* (i.e., singing without musical instruments). Members believe
that the use of instruments is unbiblical, has no evidence in history, and is an
accommodation to wealthier members.[10]

Local churches are called churches of Christ because that is precisely
what they are—the local presence of Christ. The priesthood of all believers is
emphasized. There is a reluctance to give titles to ministers or clergy. Instead,
there are elders and deacons. In some cases, the titles shepherd, bishop, minister, or pastor may be used. Some of these may be women.

There is no recognized organization beyond the local church. When attempts are made to organize interchurch activities or groups, serious debate
ensues over whether or not the plan is biblical.[11]

Churches of Christ have several categories. A large percentage follows
the teachings of the Restoratation Movement without anything out of the
ordinary for the movement. However, some smaller groups have unique
features. For example, the "one cup" group of approximately 550 congregations use one cup instead of many in the Lord's Supper. Approximately 1,100

---

[10] Churches of Christ use the following verses to support worship without instruments: Matthew 26:30; Romans 15:9; Ephesians 5: 18-19; 1 Corinthians 14:15; Colos-
sians 3:16 and Hebrews 2:12.

[11]Some Churches of Christ have been known to reject ecumenical activities, such as
Billy Graham crusades because true churches, according to the Churches of Christ,
are not supposed to mix with false Christians (i.e., non-Churches of Christ members).
Moreover, churches are supposed to be autonomous and never work with each other. For an example, see Garland Elkins, "Which Church," *Yokefellow* 31:5 (May, 2004),
pp. 1-2.

churches do not have Bible classes or Sunday schools because these cannot be found in the Bible and are recent innovations.

### The Independent Christian Churches/Churches of Christ

Located primarily in the Midwest and South, these churches do not want to be identified with either the Christian Church (Disciples of Christ) or the Churches of Christ. They are normally called Christian churches without the word "Independent" in their names. They often use their location as part of their titles, such as Southeast Christian Church Louisville, Kentucky. The movement has 52 mega churches with over 2,000 members each.[12]

Four popular slogans mark this group of churches:

- Where the scriptures speak, we speak; where scriptures are silent, we are silent.
- In essentials unity, in opinions liberty, in all things love.
- No headquarters but heaven; no creed but Christ; no book but the Bible, no plea but the gospel, and no name but the divine.
- Christians only, but not the only Christians.
- Locally autonomous

Independent Christian Churches/Churches of Christ have no creeds. Instead, they believe that the Bible is the sole standard for faith and practice. Independent Christian Churches can choose to have a belief or practice even if the Bible does not clearly say so or imply these.

These Restorationists have weekly communion on the "first day of the week" and their non-liturgical worship includes both instrumental and vocal music. They practice believers' baptism after expressing repentance and faith.

Local churches are directed by elders, normally all male. While recognizing no authority beyond the local church, they operate through networks of established ministries and churches. This category of Restorationists has a variety of colleges and seminaries, such as Milligan College, Florida Christian College, and Kentucky Christian College.

### The Disciples of Christ/The Christian Church

This Restorationist group of approximately one million members has traditionalist and modernist members in local churches. Famous members have included former presidents Lyndon Baines Johnson and Ronald Reagan, Jim Jones of the People's Temple, Colonel Sanders of the Kentucky Fried Chicken franchise, and Episcopal Bishop Gene Robinson.

---

[12] Two prominent examples are Southeast Christian Church with 18,000 plus members and Central Christian Church in Las Vegas, Nevada with 11,000 plus members.

This movement has no creed. It respects creeds formulated in Christian history, but these creeds have no binding authority. Typical of Restoration-ists, the Bible, in particular the New Testament, is the sole authority for mat-ters of belief and practice.

The community is split over how to see and interpret the Bible. Some say that the Bible bears witness to Christ and that it is fallible. Others say that the Bible is the infallible, inspired Word of God. Members of the group believe that people are sinful and need Christ, although they do not believe that sin is inherited from Adam. Because of their mix of traditionalists and modernists, the Disciples of Christ disagree about many significant social issues. But, because each church is self-governing, they can have this diversity without splitting from each other.

Congregational worship is non-liturgical and includes instrumental and vocal music. Baptism is for believers only and is done by immersion. The Lord's Supper is celebrated weekly as a memorial.

These Restorationists believe in the priesthood of all believers. Lay elders preside over the Lord's Table. They and pastors provide spiritual oversight for congregational members.

Although each congregation is independent and self-governing, the Dis-ciples of Christ have regional, national, and international structures. A general assembly and general assembly president direct denominational ministries. In 2005 CE, *Reverend Dr. Sharon Watkins* was elected as the first woman president of a mainline denomination. The Disciples of Christ believe that they should work with other churches in the same movement and with others outside of Restorationism. They recognize that a national/international church exists, although they deny that institution any authority. The Disciples support a network of schools, colleges, and other agencies to improve society.[13] They maintain residence halls on many college and university campuses.[14]

An example of how this denomination is split between traditionalists and liberals has to do with how it has handled same-sex marriages. The Indianap-olis-based denomination does not have an official policy on same-sex unions. Its congregational polity has contributed to a tenuous denominational work-ing dynamic on this issue.

Events highlight the unsettled situation in the denomination. Operating from a 1997 CE General Assembly resolution that called for the enactment of legislation that would terminate the denial of civil rights based on sexual ori-entation, the denomination as a whole is in a discernment process over the

---

[13] Some colleges and universities include Hiram, Eureka, Lynchburg and Transylvania Colleges and Texas Christian University. Numbered among the group's theological schools are Brite, Christian, Phillips, and Lexington.

[14] Disciples Divinity Houses can be found at Vanderbilt University and the University of Chicago.

question of supporting same-sex unions. The Assembly asked the church to consider the role of gays and lesbians in the life of the church.

In 1998 CE, the denomination's Administrative Committee called for the development of a discernment process that congregations could use to engage the question. After spending 3 years listening to the positions of church members, a 16 member committee gave an address at the 2001 CE Assembly on the Process of Discernment on the Participation of Gays and Lesbians in the Life of the Christian Church (Disciples of Christ). They recommended that each local congregation begin a seven-step exploration process, called discernment. These include: an introduction, spiritual preparation, listening to stories, Bible study, telling personal stories, next steps in relating to gays and lesbians, and consecration.

The *National City Christian Church* in Washington, D. C. voted to allow same-sex unions on December 7, 2002 CE after a gay couple requested that the church's pastor, Alvin O. Jackson, bless their relationship. In January 2003 CE, traditionalists within the denomination called on the church to change its decision. Doug Harvey, Executive Director of *Disciple Renewal* (now *Disciples Heritage Fellowship*), called on the church to "either rescind the decision or end its unique relationship with the denomination."[15]

Since then, given the congregational government of the denomination, different churches and localities have taken different positions on this issue. Two geographical areas have declared that they will not ordain non-celibate gays and lesbians. They are the Northeast Region (New York and New England) and the Southwest Region (Texas and New Mexico). On the other hand, the Northern California Region has announced that it is 'Open & Affirming." This title is used by the Disciples of Christ and the United Church of Christ congregations and regions to say that they welcome the full involvement of gay and lesbian people as members and clergy.

## SEE WHAT YOU KNOW ABOUT THE EMERGING CHURCH AND STONE-CAMPBELL RESTORATIONISM

1. Identify and describe four beliefs.

---

[15] "An Evangelical Group in the Christian Church Has Called on the Denomination's Flagship Congregation to Change its Recent Decision to Allow Same-Sex Unions," *The Christian Century* (1/25/2003).

2. Identify and describe three characteristics of lifestyle.

3. Identify and describe four characteristics of ceremonies.

4. Identify and describe three characteristics of institutions.

# CHAPTER IX

## ✠

# TRADITIONAL PROTESTANTISM—
# THE AMISH

Chapters Nine through Thirteen contain descriptions of several examples of traditional Protestants.

### Chapter Nine
- The Amish

### Chapter Ten
- Holiness and the Salvation Army

### Chapter Eleven
- Fundamentalism
- Evangelicalism

### Chapter Twelve
- Pentecostalism
- The Charismatic Movement

### Chapter Thirteen
- Mega Churches

### The Amish

One of the most famous and respected religious groups in North America is the Amish. Tourists travel to *Lancaster, Pennsylvania*, where the largest concentration of Amish live, to observe their quaint, rural "horse and buggy" lifestyle. The Amish have been portrayed with some degree of favorability in movies with Harrison Ford and Tim Allen.[1] Yet, for the most part, few really understand why the Amish have chosen to live like they do. In fact, most are first to say that while they admire the Amish, they would never wish to live like them.

The "English" (all non-Amish) are often confused by the bewildering variety of names of Amish sects and by the diverse terms that even the Amish use to name themselves. Some names include: House-Amish, Church-Amish, Black-Bumper Mennonite, Thirty-Fivers, Black-Buggy Mennonites, Hook-and-Eye Amish, Automobile Amish, New Order Amish, Swartzentruber Amish, Andy Weaver Amish, and Beachy Amish. The largest Amish group is the *Old Order Amish*. This is the subject of the discussion that follows.

The Amish are part of a broader category of contemporary religious communities that stem from the Anabaptist Movement during the Protestant Reformation. These include the Hutterites, the Bruderhof Communities, and more traditional sections of the Brethren and Mennonite faiths. Whether or not these faith communities actually are genetic descendants of the original Anabaptists may not be clearly established, however, they all reflect the teaching and ethos of the original Anabaptists (see Chapter Six).

### Beliefs

The beliefs and practices of the Amish are based on the writings of one of the founders of the Mennonite faith, *Menno Simons* (1496-1561 CE). Having previously been parts of one movement, the Amish and Mennonite split in the 17th century CE when the former came to believe that the Mennonites had a lack of discipline, especially in regard to the *Meidung* or shunning. The movement's founder was Jacob Amman.

The Amish seek to imitate God in the way that they think and act. To accomplish this, the community seriously seeks to establish a holy life by adopting a 15th century CE lifestyle with a few minor modifications. They separate themselves from outsiders (i.e., the *English*), while leading an active family and community life with strict observance of community rules (i.e., the *Ordnung*).

For the Amish, the Bible is the inspired, infallible Word of God, which is taken quite literally. In addition to the sacred texts, there are many unwritten rules or the Ordnung, which while not specified in writing are known and closely followed.

Important beliefs among the Amish are humility (Demut) and Gelassenheit (calmness, composure, placidity), a "letting-be," a willingness not to promote oneself.

### Ways of Life

The Amish also are willing to follow what God says in ways that separate them from contemporary cultural norms. The Amish believe that this separa-

---

[1] Harrison Ford was the lead in the 1985 movie *Witness* (Paramount) and Tim Allen co-starred with Kristie Alley in the 1997 movie *For Richer or Poorer* (Universal).

tion is a way to follow the Bible's teaching from James 4:4, which states, "friendship with the world is enmity with God."[2] It is also a means by which the Amish do not let themselves be conformed to the surrounding cultural ethos.

Old Order Amish have many practices that other Amish may or may not practice. Most Amish are tri-lingual. Members speak in a German dialect called Pennsylvania Dutch (Deutsch), use High German in worship and learn English in school.

Formal education beyond eighth grade is discouraged and not required, according to the United States Supreme Court (*Wisconsin vs. Yoder, 1972*). Schools are one-room buildings run by the Amish.[3]

Old Order Amish do not permit car, truck, or farm tractor ownership. However, they will ride in cars if necessary. The Amish do not use electricity or radios, TVs, personal computers, or computer games. Home phones are not allowed, but some families have phones away from the house or use the phones of non-Amish neighbors. Old Order Amish do not pay or collect Social Security, unemployment insurance, or welfare. They have a mutual aid fund for members who need help with medical costs. However, the Amish pay taxes.

Old Order Amish do not take photos or allow photos to be taken of them. This would be prideful and vain. It would break the commandment Exodus 20:4, "You shall not make for yourself any graven image or any likeness of anything that is in the earth."

### Rituals

Some groups practice *Rumspringa* or "Running Around." The purpose of this is to make sure that Amish young people really want to be committed members of the community and experience baptism. Teenagers 16 and above are permitted to have some freedom in behavior while still living at home. They may date, go out with friends, visit the outside world, go to parties, drink alcohol, and wear jeans. Typically, 80-90% of Amish youngsters decide to remain Amish.[4]

---

[2] "Adulterers! Do you not know that friendship with the world is enmity with God? Therefore whoever wishes to be a friend of the world becomes an enemy of God," NRSV (1989).

[3] Recent notoriety was brought to one-room Amish schoolhouses with the October 2, 2006 CE shootings at a particular Amish schoolhouse in Pennsylvania. For more information, see Donald B. Kraybill, Steven M. Nolt, and David L. Weaver-Zercher, *Amish Grace: How Forgiveness Transcended Tragedy* (San Francisco: Jossey-Bass, 2007).

[4] For more information, see Tom Schachtman, *Rumspringa: To Be and Not to Be Amish* (New York: North Point Press, 2006). This book is based on the 2002 Documentary Film, "The Devil's Playground" by Stick Figure Productions and directed by Lucy Walker. The film traces the experience of Amish teenagers from LaGrange County, Indiana during Rumspringa.

Meidung or shunning is the excommunication and then, the community avoidance of the unrepentant in hopes that they repent. This is done to maintain community purity and holiness and is based on 1 Corinthians 5:11.[5]

For minor infractions, the matter is taken up by both congregational leadership and regular members after a regular worship service.[6] Only community members may participate. The guilty appear, and ask forgiveness and promise to act more appropriately.

When excommunication is likely, again the leadership and congregation together choose shunning. Later on, if the shunned chooses to return to the community, they appear before the community, which then votes for re-admittance. If approved, the shunned confesses their sins, promises to stop them and then is allowed back into the fellowship. They receive handshakes, hugs, and holy kisses from members of the same sex.

The Old Order Amish hold bi-weekly worship services on alternate Sundays. On in-between Sundays, members attend services of other congregations or visit with friends or family. Services are held in the homes of the members because the Amish do not build churches or meetinghouses.

Meetings begin at 8:30 A.M. and last about three hours. The Amish sit on a set of benches that are taken from house to house for meetings. Men sit in the front rows and women in the back. Married and unmarried are separated with young unmarried often in another room

Prior to the service, community leaders gather in a room to divide up service responsibilities while the congregation beings to sing. Singing is carried out in unison and without musical instruments (i.e., a cappella). When singing, a leader starts each line by setting the pitch and singing the first syllable alone, and then the congregation joins in unison. Then the leader goes to the second line and so on. The Amish believe that their hymns were written by Anabaptist prisoners as they experienced torture and martyrdom during the Reformation. Their hymns are found in the *Ausbund* (1564 CE), which contains only verses and no musical notes.

After these activities, Amish leaders enter the room for services. At the end of the hymn singing, one leader delivers a short sermon ("Making the Start" or "Making the Beginning"). A group prayer follows with all on bended knee and afterward all stand to hear the Bible read. A long sermon of up to an hour follows and then testimonies are given. Baptized males may then make corrections to the sermon, using biblical support. After these, the congregation kneels again while a minister reads a prayer. Finally, a blessing is given. Whenever the name of Jesus is spoken, congregants bend their knees to follow the biblical injunction, "At the name of Jesus, every knee shall bow."

---

[5] "But now I am writing you that you must not associate with anyone who calls himself a brother but is sexually immoral or greedy, an idolater or a slanderer, a drunkard or a swindler. With such a man do not even eat" (NIV).

[6] An example of a minor infraction could be wearing clothing that is not allowed.

A communal meal is served when the service ends. This occurs in shifts with the leaders first, the older married couples second and then the youngest. Men and women eat separately.

Communion services are held twice yearly, in the spring and fall. Two weeks prior to each service, a required community assembly is held. During this time, disagreements are resolved so that everyone is prepared spiritually for the service.

On communion day, the Amish are supposed to fast and pray before the ritual. Communion occurs after a regular service. A minister preaches a sermon until 3:00 P.M. so that the actual communion occurs at the time of Christ's death. Then a minister distributes bread to the members, who receive it standing. After taking the bread, the member kneels briefly. Then a minister passes a single cup. After a prayer, they genuflect. They Amish practice closed communion.

At the communion service, the Amish practice foot washing. They believe that they should do this just as Jesus did in John 13. A minister reads this passage. Then the ministers bring in pails of water and the members in pairs and divided by sex, wash each other's feet. After each pair has finished, they shake hands and kiss each other. Following this, each member makes his or her semiannual offering to the church.

On their baptismal day, the candidates are seated with church leaders with boys in front of the girls or on opposite sides of the room. The baptismal service follows the long sermon after the minister has read the story of Philip and the Ethiopian (Acts 8) and has again questioned the candidates about the Amish faith. Candidates then kneel while another minister brings a bucket of water. A minister extends his hands over the candidate as the other minister pours water into the cupped hands of a minister and onto the head of the candidate. This is repeated three times. A minister then helps the male candidates to their feet and gives them his hand and kisses them. When a woman is baptized, a minister's wife assists by removing the woman's prayer cap before water is poured and replacing it afterward. The minister helps the woman stand up. He gives her the same greeting of welcome that he gives a man, but places her hand in his wife's and then the wife kisses the woman.

Amish are encouraged to marry and celibacy is not valued within the community (i.e., "Be fruitful and multiply."). Heterosexual, not homosexual, relations are the norm and are what the Bible teaches. Young men and women begin their search for a mate/marriage partner when they turn 16, and that search only occurs within the Amish community.

Typically the Amish are married by their early twenties. Before this takes place, both must be baptized members of the Amish faith and both must be following the Bible and the Ordnung. The young man asks the women to marry him, but does not give her a diamond. Instead, he presents her with something practical and useful, such as a clock or a set of china. The couple then keeps their intentions secret until July or August, when the woman tells her family of her future plans.

In late October, the names of couples planning to wed are made public on the second Sunday after the Fast Day or St. Michael's Day, typically on October 11.[7] Fathers then reveal the date and time, and invite members to attend. Couples do not attend the Amish meeting on the Sunday they are published. Instead, the women prepare meals for their intendeds and they eat together alone. When her family returns from the service, the daughters formally introduce their future husbands to their parents.

The Amish have wedding parties, but they do not have a best man or a maid (matron) of honor. All members of the wedding party are considered equals.

Ceremonies are held from late November to the middle of December to avoid planting, harvest, and winter weather. They occur on Tuesdays and Thursdays. Mondays, Wednesdays, and Fridays are used to prepare for or clean up after. Sundays are the Sabbath and are never used for weddings.

A wedding ceremony normally begins prior to daybreak after chores are completed. By 7:00 A.M., the wedding party has already eaten and dressed. They then wait in the kitchen to greet incoming guests who might number 200-400.

*Forgeher* (normally four married couples) act as ushers, assisting people to find seating on long wooden benches. At 8:30 A.M., the three-hour service begins. The congregation sings hymns without instrumental accompaniment, while the minister gives advice to the couple in another room. After this, with the minister, couple, and attendees present, a prayer, Scripture reading, and a lengthy sermon are given. Then, the minister asks the couple to step forward and he asks questions about their intentions. With this done, the minister offers a blessing and then other ordained men and the fathers voice their support of the wedding. A final prayer is offered.

Celebration follows the wedding ceremony. Women go to the kitchen to make final food preparations, while men set up tables in a u-shaped pattern in the bride's family home. A corner of the table, the *Eck* (i.e., corner), is reserved for the couple and their bridal party. The bride sits on the groom's left just like she will in the buggy. After dinner, the afternoon is spent visiting, playing games, and matchmaking.

The couple's first night together takes place at the bride's family home. They get up very early the next day to do chores and to clean the house. During the winter months, the newlyweds visit relatives on the weekends and collect their wedding presents. The couple lives with the bride's parents until they can set up their own home in the spring.

---

[7] Fasting is an important component of Amish religious life. On October 11 each year, the community fasts by at least skipping breakfast. On this day of rest, businesses are closed.

At death, the body is normally given to a non-Amish embalmer. Males are often covered with a white shawl and women normally wear their wedding gown. Caskets are plain, varnished wood lined with plain cloth. They open from the middle to expose just the waist up of the deceased. Funerals are held in the home of the deceased without a eulogy or flowers. They are like regular church services and are followed by a meal. A simple tombstone marks the grave and cemeteries can be found on farmland donated for this purpose. After death, the deceased's property is almost always retained by the family members. Because of the cost of land, it is becoming an increasing problem for younger generations to have enough land to support a family even if that land has been inherited. The Amish frequently remarry after the death of a spouse. These marriages occur outside the wedding season and have much less of a party atmosphere. Remarriage normally does not occur until at least one year after a spouse's death out of a sign of respect for the dead.

### Institutions

Many Amish came to the United States beginning in the 18th century CE and settled in Pennsylvania, New York, Illinois, Indiana, Iowa, Missouri, Ohio, Kentucky, and Tennessee. While membership numbers are hard to determine, estimates suggest that there are 150,000-180,000 members in the United States.[8] Because of large families, the Amish have a very high growth rate at 6.8 children per family.[9]

The Amish have congregational government with no formal national head office or leadership. They have geographic districts based on the locations of Amish sects. Old Order Amish local communities are made up of 25-30 neighboring farms and/or related families.

There are four church offices, all reserved for men:

- Volliger Diener (Full Servant or Bishop):   This man provides spiritual leadership for the congregation. He preaches, baptizes, marries, and ordains. He pronounces excommunication. He usually serves over one district, but may have two.

---

[8] Counting the number of Amish is a difficult task because of the lack of record-keeping or at least public record-keeping. Estimates range from 123,000 (1992) to 227,000 (2008) for Old Order Amish alone. This suggests an increasing number of Amish. For more information, see Donald B. Kraybill and C. Nelson Hostetter, *Anabaptist World USA* (Scottdale, PA: Herald Press, 2001).

[9] Julia A. Ericksen; Eugene P. Ericksen, John A. Hostetler, Gertrude E. Huntington (July 1979). "Fertility Patterns and Trends among the Old Order Amish." *Population Studies* (33), pp. 255-76.

- Diener zum Buch
  (Servant of the Book or
  Minister):

  This man assists the bishop in preaching and teaching. Most congregations have two ministers.

- Armendiener
  (Servant of the Poor
  or Deacon):

  This man reads from the Bible at church services, assists the bishops in different duties and administers funds for the poor.

Candidates for leadership positions are elected following this order:

- A pool of candidates is chosen by the votes of men and women from the congregation.
- Lots are then drawn to see which of the candidates will be chosen. This is normally done at the close of a regular worship service. As many Bibles as there are candidates are laid on a table. They all look alike. In one of these a slip of paper with a Bible verse is found. Each nominee selects one Bible and presents it to the bishop, who then opens each Bible until the one with the slip with the Bible verse is found. That determines who is elected. Immediately afterward, the chosen person is ordained.

There are no special requirements for leaders, who are chosen for life. Because of the latter, there are very few opportunities for non-leaders to assume the mantle of leadership. Bishops and others become very powerful community members and play a large religious and social role within the community.

## SEE WHAT YOU KNOW ABOUT THE AMISH

1. Identify and describe four beliefs.

2. Identify and describe three characteristics of lifestyle.

3. Identify and describe four characteristics of ceremonies.

4. Identify and describe three characteristics of institutions.

# CHAPTER X
⚔
# TRADITIONAL PROTESTANTISM—
# HOLINESS AND THE SALVATION ARMY

## Holiness

In 19th century CE America, both before and after the Civil War, the Holiness Movement was born. Leaders included Phoebe Palmer, William Boardman, Hannah Whithall Smith and Robert Pearsall Smith.

As opposed to other Christians that understand sanctification as a lifetime process, Holiness believers teach that sanctification is an instantaneous experience subsequent to salvation. This experience makes humans love God completely so that the faithful are under the control of God in their thoughts and actions. They named this experience Christian perfection or entire sanctification.

Holiness people stress the Bible's command, "Be holy as I am holy." They believe that Holiness comes from separating oneself from the evil world, which constantly attempts to lure the devout away from this holy life. Holiness people believe that holy actions should replace unholy ones and they constantly strive to carry these out.

In their striving for holiness, the faithful avoid illicit drugs, alcohol, tobacco, bad language, gambling, attending movies, dancing, and even swimming with members of the opposite sex. Children do not participate in physical education classes because gym clothes do not cover enough skin.

It is very important that women are holy. They wear no makeup and have long hair and clothes that cover almost their entire bodies. Women generally wear dresses, not slacks and definitely not shorts.

Holiness people marry within their groups and their children play with fellow members. Divorce is discouraged and marriage is stressed. Males are heads of families and having as many children as possible is encouraged.

Some churches represented in the Holiness tradition include:

- The Church of God (Cleveland, TN)
- The Church of God (Anderson, IN)
- The Churches of God in Christ
- The Mennonites
- The Church of the Nazarene
- The Wesleyan Church
- Christian and Missionary Alliance
- The Free Methodist Church
- The Salvation Army

### The Salvation Army

Most North Americans associate this movement with bell-ringing volunteers collecting money around the Christmas holidays. However, the Salvation Army is actually a holiness church founded in 1865 CE in East London by *William* and *Catherine Booth*. In 1878 CE, the movement was first called the Salvation Army. Since the mid-19th century CE, the church has spread throughout the world. Its motto is "Blood and Fire," the first being a reference to the blood of Christ shed for sins and the second being a reference to the purging fire of the Holy Spirit that is available to all.

This traditionalist group believes most of the fundamental Christian doctrines, such as the inspiration of the Bible, which is God's infallible word, the Trinity, the life, death, and resurrection of Jesus, and, justification by faith alone.

The Army emphasizes the human ability to choose salvation. And, without an active commitment to Christ, an individual can slip back into an unsaved state.

Believers should seek an experience subsequent to salvation, called *Holiness* (or Sanctification). The outcome of this deeper work of grace is demonstrated by a wholehearted commitment to Christ and his service. The Salvation Army states, "We believe that it is the privilege of all believers to be wholly sanctified, and that their whole spirit and soul and body may be preserved blameless unto the coming of our Lord Jesus Christ."[1]

Army members wear traditional clothes and refrain from activities that draw a person away from the Bible. Since they first adopted the position, "Every man and woman deserves a horse, a square meal and a place to live," the Salvation Army has focused on the needs of the poorest in society. The

---

[1] http://www.salvationarmyusa.org/usn/www_usn_2.nsf/vw-dynamic-arrays/CE33D354A0544F368025732500314AF5?openDocument

Army has had a significant ministry with alcoholics, street people, and drug addicts.

The Salvation Army does not observe ordinances or sacraments although it does have a ritual for baby dedication. Services, held in citadels or temples, are non-liturgical with hymns, prayers, testimonies, and Bible Study. The movement has a mercy seat in the front of each worship room, where the penitent can go to pray for salvation, sanctification, or some form of further commitment to Christ.

The Army is organized along military lines, adopting uniforms in 1880 CE. Military ranks are used, such as general (world leader), captain, and cadet. A person who wishes to serve in the movement becomes a soldier and in a commitment ceremony accepts their role as such by agreeing to the Army's evangelical statement of faith. From the beginning, both men and women have had equal authority. Women have been and still can be in charge of local (corps), regional, national, and international branches. Annual congresses are held. The international movement has a general and a high council.

## SEE WHAT YOU KNOW ABOUT HOLINESS AND THE SALVATION ARMY

1. Identify and describe four beliefs.

2. Identify and describe three characteristics of lifestyle.

3. Identify and describe four characteristics of ceremonies.

4. Identify and describe three characteristics of institutions.

# CHAPTER XI
## ✠
# TRADITIONAL PROTESTANTISM—
# FUNDAMENTALISM AND EVANGELICALISM

## Fundamentalism

This late 19th century CE, multi-denominational or non-denominational movement began as a reassertion of traditional Christian belief and practice in reaction to theological modernism.[1] *Modernists* sought to redefine Christianity in light of contemporary developments in the natural and social sciences.[2] In contrast to Modernism, Fundamentalists affirm the following:

- The inspiration, accuracy, and authority of the Bible
- The imminent and physical second coming of Jesus Christ with a Dispenationalist approach
- The substitutionary atonement of Jesus Christ
- The physical resurrection of Jesus Christ

---

[1] A denomination may be defined as a group of religious organizations with their own distinctive beliefs and practices. The term "multi-denominational" refers to an organization with several denominations. "Non-denominational" may be defined as a religious group which places itself outside of traditional denominational boundaries.

[2] George M. Marsden, *Fundamentalism and American Culture: The Shaping of Twentieth-Century Evangelicalism, 1870-1925*, 2nd ed. (New York: Oxford University Press, 2006); idem, *Understanding Fundamentalism and Evangelicalism* (Grand Rapids: William B. Eerdmans, 1991); Jerry Falwell, Edward Hindson and Ed Dobson *The Fundamentalist Phenomenon/The Resurgence of Conservative Christianity*, 2 ed. (Grand Rapids: Baker Publishing Group, 1986); Marla J. Selvidge (ed.), *Fundamentalism Today: What Makes It So Attractive!* (Elgin: Brethren Press, 1985); and, George W. Dollar, *A History of Fundamentalism in America* (Greenville: Bob Jones University Press, 1973).

- The virgin birth of Jesus Christ
- The "born-again" religious experience
- The use of the King James Bible as opposed to other translations
- Separatism from what they claim to be liberal churches and decadent culture
- Strict dress and social codes
- Cessationism (i.e., the gifts of the Spirit ceased to exist after the first generation of Christians and with the presence of the written word)

Early on, Fundamentalists reacted to the growing acceptance of *Biological and Social Evolutionary Theory* beginning in the mid-1800s CE. In the former, instead of the sudden and unique creation of humans as pictured in Genesis it was replaced with the notion that humans evolved over millions of years. In the latter, the notion that humans had fallen from grace and were in need of salvation was replaced with the idea that humans (and the entire social order for that matter) were getting better and better.

Add to this, the acceptance of the *Critical and Historical Approach* to studying and interpreting the Bible. In this, the Bible "presuppositionally" was treated like any other piece of literature without any divine inspiration or authority.

For followers of the emerging Fundamentalism themselves, the popularity of and focus on the second coming of Jesus Christ had an enormous impact on the movement's development by forging a network of relationships. These were created through the general use of the *Schofield Reference Bible* and through a series of popular prophetic conferences.

A particular approach to the second coming, *Dispensationalism*, became increasingly popular. Dispensationalism contended that history was divided into distinct periods or "dispensations. In each of these God acted in different ways toward his chosen people. For Fundamentalists, the current dispensation was marked by fervent anticipation for the immediate return of Christ. Coupled with this return was the notion that God's chosen people would experience the Rapture (i.e., the removal of all believers prior to the final events of the Last Days) and that the Last Days would include the rise of a one-thousand year millennial kingdom for believers, the rise of the Anti-Christ, a time of terrible suffering and cataclysmic natural events, and then the Final Judgment.

Another significant event was the publication of *The Fundamentals: A Testimony to the Truth* (1910-1915 CE), a series of 12 booklets. These were distributed to millions of pastors throughout the word. *The Fundamentals* argued for the fundamentals of faith and argued against the new beliefs on the Bible and Christian ideas as proposed by modernists. Not only did this contribute to the debate between fundamentalists and modernists by clearly delineating their differences, it also contributed to the use of the term Fundamentalism for the movement.

The era just after World War I was a watershed era for Fundamentalism. In 1919 CE, the new World's Christian Fundamentals Association's platform stated:

- A rejection of modernism in all forms
- A rejection of the theory of evolution
- The support of recently founded Bible institutes as over against established educational institutions
- A rejection of ecumenical efforts with modernist Protestants

In the 1920s CE, Fundamentalists attempted to regain control of Protestant groups which modernists controlled (most large denominations), fought for the passage of laws that supported traditional Protestant ideas (i.e., Blue Laws, Prohibition), and sought to end the teaching of evolution in public schools. Fundamentalists had some success with the last two only.

By the mid-1920s CE, because of these developments, Fundamentalism began to create its own subculture with denominations, individual churches, and educational and social institutions. Most of these distanced themselves from the broader culture.[3]

Since the 1940s CE and the separation of Evangelicals from the movement (see the following discussion on Evangelicalism), Fundamentalism has come to refer to a wide range of individuals and groups. These have included non-separatists like *Rev. Dr. Jerry Falwell* (1933-2007 CE) of Liberty Baptist University and Thomas Road Baptist Church, both in Lynchburg, Virginia. Falwell was a proud Fundamentalist, but he did not maintain a separatist agenda. He fostered relationships with non-Fundamentalists and encouraged thousands of Fundamentalists to be active politically.

On the political scene, Falwell founded the *Moral Majority* in 1979 CE. This movement supported Pro-Life and Traditional Family Issues, sought to limit the influence of the Feminist and Gay Rights Movements, lobbied for school prayer and support for the nation of Israel.

Fundamentalists can also be strict separatists. These believers teach that any mingling with social or political culture is wrong. Separatist Fundamentalists owe their beginnings to a New Jersey minister, *Rev. Carl McIntire* (1906-2002 CE). This advocate of separatism founded the American Council of Christian Churches and the Bible Presbyterian Church to advance these views. He denounced any Fundamentalists who sought points of contact with any outsiders.

Today Separatist Fundamentalists can be found in conservative Baptist (though often called Bible Baptist, or Bible churches) denominations such as the General Association of Regular Baptists (GARBC) and the Independent Fundamental Churches of America (IFCA). Institutions associated with the latter also include *Bob Jones University* in Greenville, South Carolina and Ten-

---

[3] See Joel Carpenter, *Revive Us Again: The Reawakening of Modern Fundamentalism, 1930-1946* (Oxford, 1998).

nessee Temple in Chattanooga, Tennessee. Among their publications are *The Sword of the Lord* and *The Biblical Evangelist*.

However, even some of these individuals and groups are less separatist than in the past. For example, candidate George W. Bush spoke at Bob Jones University during the 2000 CE United States Presidential Campaign and Dr. Bob Jones III went on to appear on *Larry King Live*.[4]

Fundamentalism has made a significant contribution to American religion and today has larger numbers of Protestant Christians among its membership and in its closely related, more liberal traditional offspring, Evangelicalism, than modernists.[5]

### Evangelicalism

Evangelicalism is an umbrella term for a multi-denominational or non-denominational movement that emerged from Fundamentalism in the 1940s. Evangelicalism's most visible and influential leader has been the *Rev. Billy Graham*, possibly the most prominent Christian of the last 50 years.

The movement adheres to most of the major tenets of Fundamentalism, but has its own take on a few items:

- The use of any reliable Bible translations with a special emphasis on *The New International Version* (NIV)
- Anti-separatism
- May or may not be cessationists
- Ecumenical Spirit with other Christian groups, such as Roman Catholicism, Eastern Christians, and a wide range of Protestants
- Wide-ranging ideas about appropriate dress and activities
- Active involvement in social concerns
- Judicious use of Biblical criticism and modern methods of biblical interpretation

Currently there have been at least three ways suggested to define Evangelicalism. The first approach has been taken by British historian David Bebbington. He has argued that the movement has four marks:

---

[4] Dr. Bob Jones III appeared on *Larry King Live* on March 3, 2000 CE.
[5] For information on Evangelicalism, see the material following Fundamentalism in this chapter.

According to recent research conducted on "Church Statistics and Religious Affiliations—U. S. Religious Landscape Study," by the Pew Forum on Religion and the Public Life, 26.3% of Americans label themselves Evangelicals and 18.1% consider themselves members of mainline Protestant churches. However, the percentage of evangelicals is even larger because of several groups listed as mainline which are evangelical. See http://religions.pewforum.org/affiliations

- Conversionism: The stress on individual transformation through a "born-again" experience.

- Activism: The idea that the Gospel compels believers to be involved in and transform society.

- Biblicism: An emphasis on the accuracy and authority of the Bible.

- Crucicentrism: An emphasis on Christ's sacrificial death[6]

A second tact maintains that Evangelicalism is a name given to a partnership formed during World War II. This alliance arose in reaction to what was perceived as Fundamentalism's anti-intellectual, separatist, belligerent nature. Important names here have been *Dr. Harold John Ockenga* (1905-1985 CE), Rev. Billy Graham (1918- CE), *Wheaton College, Gordon-Conwell and Fuller Theological Seminaries, Youth for Christ* and other para church organizations.[7]

A final suggestion on defining Evangelicalism has contended that the term is defined by membership in several prominent Evangelical organizations. These organizations include:

- The National Association of Evangelicals (NAE)
- The World Evangelical Alliance (WEA)

The NAE was founded in 1942 CE and today has over 50 member denominations and includes member churches from 24 other Protestant denominations. The organization believes that it represents about 30 million people.[8]

The WEA was founded in 1951 CE.[9] Its members include churches in 127 nations and over 100 international organizations. The WEA claims to represent over 420 million people.[10]

---

[6] See David Bebbington, *Evangelicalism in Modern Britain: A History from the 1730s to the 1980s* (London: Unwin Hyman, 1989), pp. 2-17.
[7] Para-church groups are those Christian groups that are "outside of official church" structures.
[8] For more information, see the NAE website at http://www.nae.net/
[9] For the pre-history of the WEA, see http://www.worldevangelicals.org/aboutwea/history.htm
[10] For more information, see the WEA website http://www.worldevangelicals.org/

## SEE WHAT YOU KNOW ABOUT FUNDAMENTALISM
## AND EVANGELICALISM

1. Identify and describe four beliefs.

2. Identify and describe three characteristics of lifestyle.

3. Identify and describe four characteristics of ceremonies.

4. Identify and describe 4 characteristics of institutions.

# CHAPTER XII

✠

# TRADITIONAL PROTESTANTISM—
# PENTECOSTALISM AND THE
# CHARISMATIC MOVEMENT

## Pentecostalism

Pentecostalism is an umbrella term for those movements within traditional Protestantism that teach that every Christian can and should have a *Baptism of the Holy Spirit* or *the Second Blessing*. This typically occurs after salvation and its "initial evidence" is speaking in tongues. This Second Blessing copies the experience of the early Church in Acts 2, when the disciples received a dramatic filling of the Holy Spirit on the Jewish Day of Pentecost.

Several significant events were of prime importance for the development of the Pentecostal movement. At a January 1, 1901 CE prayer meeting held at Bethel Bible College, Topeka, Kansas, many came to the conclusion that speaking in tongues was available in their time and that this gift was a sign of the Baptism of the Holy Spirit.

Then, in 1906 CE, Afro-American William J. Seymour's preaching helped launch the *Azuza Street Revival*, in Los Angeles. This revival received international attention and many people were drawn to it and Pentecostalism. Almost all Pentecostal groups today trace their heritage back to the Azuza Street Revival meetings.

Today's approximately 115-130 million Pentecostals worldwide are part of three groups:

- Wesleyan Holiness
- Higher Life
- Oneness[1]

---

[1] When Charismatics are included, the number of Pentecostals rises to about one-

Examples of the first include the Church of God in Christ (COGIC) and the International Pentecostal Holiness Church. Higher Life communities include the Assemblies of God and the International Church of the Four-square Gospel.[2] The most prominent Oneness groups are the United Pentecostal Church (UPCI) and the Pentecostal Assemblies of the World (PAW).[3]

Pentecostals believe many of the same things that other traditional Protestants do with few added doctrines. One of the largest groups, the Assemblies of God, has these in its "Fundamental Truths." Traditional views include: the inspiration of God, the Trinity, the deity of Christ, Trust in Jesus for salvation, the second coming of Jesus, and the ordinances of believer's baptism and communion. An important additional belief is the Baptism of the Holy Spirit with the evidence of speaking in tongues.

Pentecostals believe that the supernatural *Gifts* mentioned in the New Testament are available for use by believers today. Some of these gifts include: healing, miracles, administration, exorcism, and wisdom.

*Speaking* and *Interpretation of Tongues* (i.e., glossolalia) are two of the most prominent gifts to outsiders. Under the direction of the Holy Spirit, a Pente-

---

quarter of the world's two billion Christians. See "Pentecostalism," Pew Forum on Religion and Public Life at http://pewforum.org/docs/?DocID=140

[2] The mainly Afro-American Church of God in Christ is the largest Pentecostal church in the United States with over 5.5 million members (See "Pentecostalism," *The Columbia Encyclopedia*, 6th ed. (2008) http://www.encyclopedia.com/doc/1E1-Pentcstl.html)

For more information on the COGIC, see http://www.cogic.com/

For more information on the International Pentecostal Holiness Church (IPHC), see http://www.iphc.org/

The Assemblies of God is the largest Pentecostal denomination in the world with over 57 million members. For more information, see http://ag.org/top/

For more information on the International Church of the Foursquare Gospel, see http://www.foursquare.org/

The largest individual Protestant church in the world is the Pentecostal Yoido Full Gospel Church in Seoul, Korea with 780,000 members as of 2003 (See http://www.oikoumene.org/en/member-churches/church-families/pentecostal-churches.html)

[3] Oneness groups have a different understanding of the Trinity than their fellow Pentecostals and other Christians. They believe that "God is one, but in three manifestations" as opposed to "God is one, but in three persons." Because God's manifestation in the New Testament is Jesus Christ, all beliefs and actions must be carried out in the name of Jesus only. As a result, these Oneness groups baptize believers (not infants) by immersion in the name of Jesus only, not in the name of the Father, Son and Holy Ghost.

For more information on the United Pentecostal Church (UPCI), see http://www.upci.org/

For more information on the Pentecostal Assemblies of the World (PAW), see http://www.pawinc.org/

costal may speak in an unknown or a known tongue. Also, there is the belief that there are two forms of tongues: an individual's private prayer language and a public tongue used in church services, which must be accompanied by the gift of interpretation of tongues.

Another "very, very small" group of Pentecostals believes that the faithful should be able to pick up poisonous snakes and drink poison without any harm as a testimony of personal faith. They base this on the last chapter of Mark's Gospel (16:16-17), where the writer instructs Christians to carry out these actions.

Whatever the Pentecostal group, a visitor can generally be assured of an emotionally charged, active style of participatory worship, where members might raise their hand, clap, or dance during worship.

### The Charismatic Movement

The Charismatic Movement is made up mostly of those who have had the Pentecostal experience, but have remained members of existing Protestant, Roman Catholic, and Eastern Orthodox groups.

The term *Charismatic* was first named by Harold Bredesen, a Lutheran minister in 1962 CE to describe this phenomenon.[4] He preferred that term as opposed to neo-Pentecostal.

The term "charismatic" comes from the Greek word "charis," which means "gift." Like Pentecostals, Charismatics believe in the present-day existence and use of the gifts of the Holy Spirit.[5]

Although Pentecostals have similar beliefs about the Baptism of the Holy Spirit, they have other differences attributable to style. For example, Charismatics generally do not believe that a person must give evidence of speaking in tongues to have received the Baptism of the Holy Spirit. Also, Charismatics may have less lifestyle restrictions about dress and entertainment and often use more contemporary worship styles.

Charismatics may be found in Eastern Orthodox, Roman Catholic, and mainline Protestant denominations. They can also be found in independent churches, where the overlap between Pentecostal and Charismatic can get quite foggy.

In recent years, neo-Charismatics have formed their own denominations, such the Vineyard Movement, Sovereign Grace, and Newfrontiers. These movements are those with Pentecostal and Charismatic belief but without any connection to Pentecostal or Charismatic churches. They may be associated with the Toronto Blessing Movement of the mid-1990s CE, where members reported an increased awareness of God's presence coupled with ecstatic prayer, healings, and laughter.

---

[4] Peter Hocken *Streams of Renewal: The Origins and Early Development of the Charismatic Movement in Great Britain* (Exeter: Paternoster, 1986), p. 184.

[5] As opposed to Cessationism, see Fundamentalism in previous chapter.

*Rev. Dennis Bennett* (1917-1991 CE), an American Episcopalian, is often credited as one of the Charismatic Movement's most important influences. While
rector (minister) of St. Mark's Episcopal Church in Van Nuys, California, he
experienced the Baptism of the Holy Spirit in 1960 CE. After having been asked
to resign, Bennett moved to St. Luke's Episcopal Church in Seattle, Washington,
where he served until 1981 CE. Throughout his career, along with his wife Rita,
Bennett served as a conference speaker, author, and leader for the burgeoning
movement both inside and outside the Episcopal Church.[6]

Since 1967 CE, the Charismatic Movement has taken hold in the Roman
Catholic Church. Masses and prayer meetings, both small and large, have
been marked by added vibrancy and sometimes tongues and prophecy.

The Roman Catholic Charismatic Movement is an outgrowth of a retreat
for faculty and students from Duquesne University in February 1967 CE.
Many of those in attendance claimed to have received the Baptism of the
Holy Spirit. This movement quickly spread to other Roman Catholics, for
example to those at the University of Notre Dame and the University of
Steubenville. The movement was given significant backing by *Léon Joseph
Cardinal Suenens* (1904-1996 CE), a leading cardinal in the Roman Catholic
Church and one of four moderators of the Second Vatican Council. A Char-
ismatic Mass was held at St. Peter's in 1976 CE. Three Popes, Paul vi, John
Paul ii, and Benedict xvi have all acknowledged the movement. On March 4,
1992 CE, Pope John Paul ii said:

> At this moment in the Church's history, the Charismatic Renewal can
> play a significant role in promoting the much-needed defense of Chris-
> tian life in societies where secularism and materialism have weakened
> many people's ability to respond to the Spirit and to discern God's loving
> call. Your contribution to the re-evangelization of society will be made in
> the first place by personal witness to the indwelling Spirit and by showing
> forth His presence through works of holiness and solidarity.[7]

### SEE WHAT YOU KNOW ABOUT PENTECOSTALISM AND THE CHARISMATIC MOVEMENT

1. Identify and describe four beliefs.

---

[6] His personal story, *Nine O'Clock in the Morning* (Gainsville: Bridge-Logos Press,
1970), had a tremendous influence inside and outside Episcopal circles.
[7] http://catholiccharismatic.us/ccc/articles/John_Paul/John_Paul_001.html

2. Identify and describe three characteristics of lifestyle.

3. Identify and describe four characteristics of ceremonies.

4. Identify and describe three characteristics of institutions.

# CHAPTER XIII

✠

# TRADITIONAL PROTESTANTS—
# MEGA CHURCHES

A recent Protestant phenomenon is the *Mega Church*. These communities of faith are large in terms of numbers (upward to 20,000 members each). Some are associated with particular religious groups (i.e., Southern Baptist), while others are independent and may have established their own denomination or association. Many, but not all mega churches are Charismatic/Pentecostal. The overall number of North Americans who go to a mega church is quite small. About five million people attend mega churches regularly.[1]

Mega churches are typically strongest in geographic areas experiencing or having just experienced growth. Regular worshippers are generally suburban, white, and younger than those in smaller congregations. However, many have members that are mostly black. Led by Bishop T. D. Jakes, one of the largest is Potter's House in Dallas, Texas with 30,000 members.

Mega churches have several consistent traits. First, most have traditional doctrines, such as an inspired, infallible Bible, the Trinity, the deity of Christ, and justification by faith. Mega churches also put very little stress on denominations, even if they are part of a particular group. A visitor would have to look very closely to see any signs of affiliation (i.e., who publishes Sunday school materials or what names are given to specific ministries in the church).

---

[1] For more information on mega churches, see the "Database of Mega churches in the United States," Hartford Institute for Religious Research, http://hirr.hartsem.edu/megachurch/database.html

Also, see Scott Thumma and Dave Travis, *Beyond Mega Church Myths: What We Can Learn from America's Largest Churches* (San Francisco: Jossey-Bass, 2007).

Mega churches have a non-threatening, cozy, and informal *Seeker Approach*. They are concerned with those who are "seekers," individuals who are un-churched, if not turned off, by organized religion. So, congregations try to figure out what these people think and how to reach them, rather than the seriously mature Christian, at least at the main worship services. Attempting to be less "churchy," they have well-produced worship services, dramatic productions and light shows, and catchy, upbeat music. Preachers preach in a folksy style. For those who are more mature in their faith, there are mid-week services and small groups.

Mega churches have many "bells and whistles" that other churches do not have. For example, Mariner's Church in Los Angeles has a coffee shop. The church website states:

Come in with friends to relax in cushy chairs, sip your favorite hot beverage, and enjoy a break from your daily grind. . . . The Global Café has brought together professionally trained chefs to design a menu that offers something for every diner. Look for much more than just coffee. How about chipotle-style fish tacos or the classic iceberg wedge with blue cheese crumbles? Hungry for made-to-order salads and sandwiches or a homemade pizza? Fresh smoothie or a Starbucks coffee drink? Check out our weekly specials for something new and different.[2]

These congregations can also provide a complete social context—sports and recreation facilities, such as basketball courts, pools, spas, and roller-skating rinks. They can have movie theaters and retirement homes.

More than mere facilities, mega churches can provide "bells and whistles" when it comes to programs, such as single groups, job fairs, vocational training, auto repair clinics, poetry writing classes, and music recording studios. Mega churches can provide big name speakers and conferences and may even own their own retreat center.

As an example, Potter's House has 59 different ministries within the church, including GED/literacy programs, AIDS outreach, homeless outreach, male mentorship, a debutante program, and a prison ministry.[3]

Finally, mega churches are in good financial shape and have plenty of volunteers.[4]

---

[2] http://www.marinerschurch.org/pages/bookstoreandcafe.html
[3] http://www.thepottershouse.org/v2/component/option,com_frontpage/Itemid,1/
[4] The subject of mega churches and money has been a popular subject for inquiry over the past 30 years. For a 2007 example in Toronto, Canada, see "Mega Church Launches an Audit," http://www.thestar.com/article/191108

Also, in 2007, Senator Charles Grassley (R-Iowa) launched an investigation into several mega churches. For more information see "Senator Probes Mega Churches' Finances," http://www.npr.org/templates/story/story.php?storyId=16860611

One of the most prominent, if not the most prominent, mega churches in North American is *Willow Creek Community Church*, a 20,000 member congregation just outside Chicago, Illinois.

The church sprang out of a popular youth ministry sponsored by South Park Church, South Ridge, Illinois, which used drama, music, and Bible teaching to reach over 1,000 teens weekly. In time, some of those involved in this youth work decided to found a church. On October 12, 1975 CE, this fellowship began in a movie theater with 125 present. Within 3 years, attendance had grown to over 2,000. In 1977 CE, property was purchased in South Barrington and in 1981 CE, services were first held there. Since then, the congregation has grown and so have the facilities. Soon, Willow Creek was influencing others with the establishment of the *Willow Creek Association*, which has churches that cross denominational lines and geographic locations.

On its attractive website, chief pastor Bill Hybels states:

> Welcome to Willow Creek Church, where our doors are wide open to people from all backgrounds. What visitors usually notice first is the large number of people who attend our weekly services and the more than 100 ministries that meet a wide range of needs. Our size has benefits: we're big enough for you to blend in and investigate the claims of Jesus Christ anonymously . . . In many ways we are small. In fact, we are actually a network of small groups . . . Together we're striving to become the kind of church described in the Bible . . . So whether you're a spiritual seeker . . . or a committed Christian . . you can find a home at Willow Creek.[5]

Willow Creek's list of beliefs are aligned with traditionalist Protestantism, such as beliefs in the Trinity, the deity of Jesus, the inspiration and errorless Bible, and justification by faith alone. The church accepts believers' baptism by immersion or sprinkling.

Until recently, Willow Creek Church pioneered the use of seeker services. In line with the seeker approach, the church had a webpage and a special ministry devoted to them. The church's seeker ministry provided for what the church understood to be the felt needs of baby boomers: messages that reflect a nurturing, forgiving God who cares about the concerns of isolated and hectic suburban life (i.e., a focus on the benefits of being a Christian as over against the requirements). Willow Creek sponsored small groups for seekers who met to discuss some of the big questions of faith without judgment and where people can learn what the Bible says about these issues (i.e., Does God exist?, Is the Bible true?, Is there one way to God?).

---

[5] http://www.willowcreek.org/welcome.asp

In a recent self-study, Willow Creek Church argued that while its seeker approach has been very successful, its believer ministry has been weak.[6] As a result, the church has moved away from its seeker approach and has begun to focus on helping committed believers advance in their faith.[7]

Mega churches differ on whether or not women should be pastors or elders. Willow Creek has had women in these positions from the beginning and made a clear commitment to continuing this practice.

## SEE WHAT YOU KNOW ABOUT MEGA CHURCHES

1. Identify and describe four beliefs.

2. Identify and describe three characteristics of lifestyle.

---

[6] See Greg Hawkins and Cally Parkinson, *Reveal: Where are You?* (Barrington: Willow Creek Association, 2007). For an analysis of this study, see "What Reveal Reveals: Criticisms of Willow Creek's Latest Self-Study Do Not Undermine Its Value" *Christianity Today* 52:3 (March, 2008) at http://www.christianitytoday.com/ct/2008/march/11.27.html

[7] For more information, see Matt Branaugh, "Willow Creek's 'Huge Shift'," *Christianity Today* (May 5, 2008).

3. Identify and describe four characteristics of ceremonies.

4. Identify and describe three characteristics of institutions.

# CHAPTER XIV
✠
# LIBERAL PROTESTANTS

There are very few examples of free-standing modernist Protestant groups. Most Protestant modernists are members of existing Protestant groups, such as Methodist, Presbyterian and Episcopal communities.

### United Fellowship of Metropolitan Community Churches (MCC)

An example of a free-standing Modernist Protestant denomination is the United Fellowship of Metropolitan Community Churches (MCC), a Protestant religious community for gay, lesbian, and transgender individuals.[1]

MCC history began when a defrocked 27 year old Pentecostal preacher, Rev. Troy Perry, felt that he received a call to found a church that affirmed gays, lesbians, and transgendered people. The MCC was established on October 6, 1968 CE, when Perry and 11 men and women held a worship service and established a church in Los Angeles. Jews, heterosexuals, a Latino, Protestants, and Roman Catholics attended this service. Since its founding, the MCC has grown and now includes over 300 churches in 18 nations. In 2000, there were about 40,000 members. In small communities, the local MCC may be the only gay or lesbian organization.

The MCC affirms many traditional teachings of Protestant Christianity, such as the Trinity, the life, death and resurrection of Jesus, the Holy Spirit, and justification by faith alone. Metropolitan Community Churches believe that the Bible is the sole authority for faith and practice.

However, the MCC has adopted some positions that put them at variance with the rest of Christianity. The church teaches that because God created homosexuals and heterosexuals alike, he accepts both and their sexual activities equally. Those biblical passages that have been used to condemn

---

[1] For more information, see http://www.mcchurch.org/AM/Template.cfm?Section=Home

homosexuality either have been misinterpreted or belong to a less tolerant age. Earlier misinterpretations or anti-gay texts are not applicable to our time when many have come to accept homosexuality as an alternative lifestyle. The Metropolitan Community Churches focus on biblical passages that stress God's acceptance, tolerance, and love.

Because they believe in congregational government, MCCs can be liturgical or non-liturgical. They may call their central rituals sacraments or ordinances. Infants or believers may be baptized. Gay and lesbian couples may have marriage ceremonies in these churches.

### SEE WHAT YOU KNOW ABOUT LIBERAL PROTESTANTS

1. Identify and describe four beliefs.

2. Identify and describe three characteristics of lifestyle.

3. Identify and describe four characteristics of ceremonies.

4. Identify and describe three characteristics of institutions.

# CHAPTER XV

✠

# CHURCH, SECT, AND CULT PROTESTANTISM

A second way to divide Protestantism is to use the three-fold sociological division, *Church, Sect,* and *Cult.* This model had its origins in the studies of Max Weber and his colleague Ernest Troeltsch and was popularized first in America by H. Reinhold Niebuhr.[1] The fundamental idea is that religious groups fall along a spectrum, ranging from those that stand close to existing social and religious culture and those that move in varying degrees away from these cultures. The term cult has been added to this continuum along with other labels, such as denomination.

## Church Protestantism
Elements of this branch of Protestantism include:

- It is the most well-known version of the faith.
- It has educated, credentialed clergy.
- It has membership from all social classes.
- It is closely allied with the state and political powers.
- It has no beliefs or practices that set it apart from the culture in which it finds itself.
- It is the guardian of religious orthodoxy.

---

[1] See Max Weber, *The Protestant Ethic and the Spirit of Capitalism* (1904); and Ernest Troeltsch, *The Social Teaching of the Christian Churches* (1911); H. Richard Niebuhr, *The Social Sources of Denominationalism* (1929); Roy Wallis, *The Road to Total Freedom: A Sociological Analysis of Scientology* (New York: Columbia University Press, 1977); Rodney Stark (ed.) *Religious Movements: Genesis, Exodus, Numbers* (New York: Paragon House, 1985); John A. Saliba, *Understanding New Religious Movements,* 2nd edition (Walnut Creek, Lanham: Alta Mira Press, 2003).

- It exercises a religious monopoly and brooks no religious competition.
- It works with other religious groups, Christian and otherwise.
- It has a bureaucracy with religious professionals.
- It gains new members generally by natural reproduction and religious socialization.
- Church Protestantism focuses on making this world a better place as opposed to issues of eternal destiny.

## Sect Protestantism

- The word sect comes from the Latin word *Sequi*, which means "to follow."
- Sects move away from the general culture and from Church Protestantism.
- Sect Protestants adhere to teachings and/or practices provided for them through the unique experiences of a founder or a group of founders.
- These teachings and/or practices are usually found in added scriptures, which are considered equal, superior or less in authority to the Bible. Examples of practices include Saturday instead of Sunday worship and separate swimming times for men and women.
- Secures new members by conversion much more than by natural reproduction.
- Sect Protestants tend to focus more on otherworldly issues, such as salvation and eternal destiny.
- The goal of ethics is to prepare sect members for eternal life along traditional lines and in as many areas of life as plausible
- Sects stress purity of doctrine and a return to original religious teaching, which has been perverted by Church Protestantism.
- Sects tend to emphasize uncredentialed lay leadership.

## Cult Protestantism (New Religious Movements)

- The word cult is a problematic word because it automatically conjures up negative feelings and images when heard. Plus, no one ever says, "I am a cult member!"
- A popular substitute for cult is New Religious Movement
- Cult Protestantism sits on the fringe of the Protestant Movement.
- Cult members reject the dominant religious models of Church Protestantism and Sect Protestantism.
- Protestant cults have many distinguishing beliefs and practices that make them quite different than their Protestant counterparts.

- Cults have an authoritarian structure, which does not allow for contributions from the rank-and-file.
- Cults are millennial, that is, they believe that the end of the world will come through their group, which will set all things right.
- Cults have messianic leaders. The group believes that their leader has arisen because only he/she can correct the problems of the world. These leaders have "messianic" complexes because they feel that God has chosen them for a special mission. This leader is normally not credentialed with "worldly credentials."
- Cults tend to focus on other-worldly concerns rather than on the this-worldly focus of Church Protestantism.

### Church, Sect, Cult: An Evaluation

This three-part model has many strengths and weaknesses. On the positive side, it allows outside observers to categorize the endless numbers of Protestant groups. There is a big difference between the Amish who drive a horse and buggy to a meeting in a home and the Methodist who drives their hot Ferrari to a beautiful church building.

On the negative side, Church Protestantism originated and defined the Church, Sect, Cult division and feels like it has the right to say which groups belong in which category. As Dr. Kathleen Flake of Vanderbilt University states, "The common definition of a cult is captured in a common joke, my faith is a religion, yours is a sect, and that guy over there whom we don't like, well, his is a cult."[2]

Add to that, what defines the most problematic word of the three, the term cult? Is a religion categorized as a cult by its distance from mainstream culture, by its highly unusual beliefs or practices, or by its connection to Christianity (i.e., a cult is any non-Christian religion)? In other words, the terms themselves have issues. Because of this terminology issue, some scholars have suggested using *New Religious Movements* instead of cult.

Finally, Protestant groups move in and out of these categories. For example, relatively few people would be unwilling to label Jim Jones's community a cult because of their ritual death by Kool-Aid poisoning. However, the People's Temple was originally part of the Disciples of Christ denomination, a major church group, and Rev. Jones was officially ordained by them.

Given all the strengths and weaknesses of these terms, they are still helpful in helping to distinguish Protestant groups one from another.

---

[2] See Kathleen Flake, "No Joke" for a critique of this tri-fold division. http://newsweek.washingtonpost.com/onfaith/kathleen_flake/2007/09/no_joke_1.html

## SEE WHAT YOU KNOW ABOUT CHURCH, SECT, AND CULT PROTESTANTISM

1. Identify and describe four traits of Church Protestantism.

2. Identify and describe four traits of Sect Protestantism.

3. Identify and describe four traits of Cult Protestantism.

# CHAPTER XVI

## ✠

# JOSEPH SMITH, JR. AND MORMON RESTORATIONISM[1]

Mormon *Restorationism* is the largest indigenous religious movement found in North America. Among its member churches are the approximately 100 or so groups that trace their roots back to the church established by *Joseph Smith, Jr.* around 1830 CE. Some of the most notable religious bodies are:

- The Church of Jesus Christ of the Latter-day Saints (*LDS*)
- The Community of Christ (formerly the Reorganized Church of Jesus Christ of the Latter Day Saints—RLDS)
- Independent RLDS/Restoration Branches
- The Fundamentalist Church of Jesus Christ of the Latter-day Saints (FLDS)
- The Church of Christ (Temple Lot)
- The Restoration Church of Jesus Christ[2]

---

[1] Joseph Smith, Jr. (1805-1844 CE) was the founder of Mormon Restorationism, whereas Joseph Smith III (1832-1914 CE), his son, became the leader of the Reorganized Church of Jesus Christ of the Latter Day Saints (now the Community of Christ). "Mormon" is a term used by the Church of Jesus Christ of the Latter-day Saints (LDS) and a few other related groups. The LDS objects to its use by any other group but themselves.

[2] See Chapter Sixteen for information on the RLDS and the FLDS.

The Independent RLDS/Restoration Branches are those groups that became independent of the RLDS in the 1980s CE as a result of the RLDS's changing beliefs and practices. It has 12,000 members in 200 plus mostly autonomous branches and study groups and a headquarters in Independence, MO. Most are either affiliated with centerplace.org and most members of the priesthood of these branches joined

All Mormon Restorationists agree that the authentic Christian church ceased to exist in the second century when its leaders discarded many of the initial teachings of Jesus Christ, Paul, and the other apostles. This "falling away" is called the *Great Apostasy*.³ In this Great Apostasy, the church lost the authority to preach the Gospel and to administer the ordinances as established by Christ and his apostles. Its leaders depended on their own knowledge of what the true Gospel was and how it was practiced. Because of this, much was forgotten.

Coupled with the Great Apostasy, is the belief that true Christianity was restored when Joseph Smith, Jr. founded the Church of Jesus Christ of the Latter-day Saints in 1830 CE. Along with this came the authority of Christ and his apostles to lead, preach and administer the missing ordinances. This has been reestablished through revelation to a Restored Priesthood with church authority.

A final belief here is in *Continuous Revelation* (i.e., God continues to speak today with as much authority as with earlier revelations).

This all began when Smith had a series of visions beginning with the "First Vision" in 1830 CE when he was visited by God the Father and Jesus. He had encounters with different angels, including Moroni from whom he received the "Everlasting Gospel." Other visitors were John the Baptist, Moses, Elijah, Peter, James, and John. Smith later testified that these messengers gave him and a man named Oliver Cowdery the authority of the priesthood so that the "Fullness of the Gospel" could now be preached with the

---

with the *Conference of Restoration Elders*. Later in 2005 CE some branches organized into a *Joint Conference of Restoration Branches*. See their Web site: conferenceofbranches.org

Founded in 1863 CE, the Church of Christ (Temple Lot) has 5,000 members and a headquarters on the Temple Lot (The Temple Lot is a two acre plot of land that was dedicated by Joseph Smith in 1831 CE as the location for the New Jerusalem or City of Zion and his place for the final gathering of the Saints in the Last Days. Today it has a non-temple building on the property that serves as the headquarters of Church of Christ-Temple Lot) in Independence, MO (For more information, see the church website: churchofchrist-tl.org).

The Restoration Church of Jesus Christ (also known as the Gay Mormon Church, the Liberal Mormon Church and at first, the Church of Jesus Christ of All Latter-day Saints) was founded in 1985 CE by Antonio Feliz and has 500 members, mostly in Utah and California. It is predominately a gay, lesbian, and transgender community

Restorationist bodies that have no direct link to Joseph Smith and the rest of Mormonism include: The Disciples of Christ, the Churches of Christ, and the Independent Christian Churches.

³ There is considerable debate over when the Great Apostasy occurred. Did it occur shortly after the death of the last apostle (around 100 CE), in the early writings of the earliest Church Fathers (100-200 CE), when obedience to bishops became the organizing standard for church practice or when the practice of infant baptism was adopted?

ordinances. This restoration included the command not to join any existing Christian group because all were in serious error and none practiced true Christianity. It also contained the reinstatement of the original Church of Christ on April 6, 1830 CE. The church teaches that it is the heir of this Church of Christ and that Smith is the successor to Peter.

All Mormon Restorationists believe that extra books of equal authority to the Bible have been added by God. However, the groups differ often on which books are considered authoritative beyond the Bible and the *Book of Mormon*.

Mormon Restorationism has two types of history: *sacred* and *real* or that which is taken on faith and that which is provable using critical historical analysis.

In the former, the prophet Mormon put together a narrative about the Lehi, who brought a group of people to North America around 600 BCE. Another story involves the Jeredites who came to North America around the time of the Tower of Babel (Genesis 11). These records are included in the *Book of Mormon*. Mormons also believe that Jesus came to North America after his resurrection to bring his truth and order to those who lived here.

After Joseph Smith's death in 1844 CE, schisms occurred in the movement and a variety of movements were established all with Restorationist characteristics. The largest group led by *Brigham Young* moved to Utah while several of the small groups remained in Missouri or moved to surrounding states.

### The Church of Jesus Christ of the Latter-day Saints (LDS)

Originally Joseph Smith's church was called the Church of Christ. To avoid any confusion with other Restorationist churches with that name, around 1852 CE, the term Church of Jesus Christ of the Latter-day Saints was adopted when the Utah branch was incorporated. The term LDS is used by this branch. Other groups of Mormon Restorationists have adopted close but different names (Reorganized Church of the Latter-Day Saints) or have coined other formal names (for example, Church of Christ-Temple Lot).

As of 2007 CE, the LDS branch of Mormon Restorationism is the largest with over 13 million members and 28,000 congregations called wards or branches. Its headquarters is in Salt Lake City, Utah. Recent estimates of church wealth have hit 30 billion dollars.[4] It has had wide exposure with a 2008 CE Republican Presidential candidate (Mitt Romney), a large hotel chain (Marriott), the 2002 CE Winter Olympics, and the church's 2008 CE support for Proposition Eight in California.

The LDS was established during the succession crisis after Smith's death in 1844 CE. Faithful Mormons asked, "Who was Smith's successor?" The LDS answer was that Smith had handed over the "keys of the kingdom" to

---

[4] David Van Biema, "Kingdom Come," *Time Magazine* (August 4, 1997).

the Quorum of Twelve Apostles and their leader, Brigham Young.[5] The majority of Mormons accepted this decision and moved to Utah to establish the LDS community under Young.

LDS teachings are found in the Bible, *The Book of Mormon*, *Doctrines and Covenants* and *The Pearl of Great Price*. The church claims that the *Book of Mormon* is equal in authority to the Bible. This fact is emphasized in numerous TV commercials, which show a Bible and the *Book of Mormon* side-by-side. However, in reality, the *Book of Mormon* trumps the Bible because where the two disagree, the former is always right.

The Mormon "Trinity" or the preferred term *Godhead* is quite unique. God the Father, God the Son, and God the Holy Spirit exist as three separate beings who are one in spirit, mind, and purpose. This is different than the traditional Christian understanding that God is one in essence, but three in persons.

Mormons feel that God and Jesus both have physical bodies, while the Holy Spirit does not. God the Father's physical body is derived from the fact that he was once a human being. A favorite Mormon quote is, "As humans are, God once was. As God is, humans can become." This points to two things: Mormons believe that God was once a human, who evolved into divinity. They also teach that humans can become gods themselves in the afterlife.

LDS references include a "Heavenly Mother" ("Mother in Heaven"), the wife of God the Father and the mother of human spirits. She is the subject of a church hymn and she is mentioned in church teaching manuals and sermons.[6] Little is said about her and many LDS members do not know about or recognize her existence.

The Latter-day Saints believe that humans have the free choice to accept or to reject their religion. Salvation comes by faith in Mormon teachings and by living a life along Mormon guidelines. In his suffering and death, Jesus provided this opportunity for individuals "to be saved" by obedience to the laws and ordinances of the Gospel.

Salvation has two forms. The first is unconditional. In this, all humans have eternal life by virtue of Christ's death. The second is conditional. In this,

---

[5] Also known as the Quorum of the Twelve, Council of the Twelve, the Twelve, or the Council of the Twelve Apostles. Joseph Smith II established this group to be one of the governing bodies of the church. They were to serve as ambassadors of the church to the world.

[6] For an example, see Joseph F. Smith, Sr. et al, "The Origin of Man," *The Improvement Era* (November, 1909), p. 80. Hymn references include: "Oh, My Father," LDS Hymn 292 and "Oh, What Songs of the Heart," LDS Hymn 286.

LDS curriculum makes mention of the Heavenly Mother. For example, see the conclusion of *The Latter Day Saint Women, Lesson 9* and *"Chapter 2: Our Heavenly Family"*, Gospel Principles, 11 (1997). See also a statement by a former President of the Church in Spencer W. Kimball, *"The True Way of Life and Salvation"*, Ensign, May 1978, p. 4.

all who believe the Gospel, repent and are baptized enter into the Kingdom of God.

At death, all spirits go to a spirit world to wait for a general resurrection of the dead and the final judgment where they will receive a new immortal, physical body. Prior to the last judgment, Jesus will return followed by a 1,000 year period and then a final battle.

During the 1,000 years of peace, Jesus will reign in two locations: one in the United States and the other in Jerusalem.[7] At this time, only those about to enter the *Celestial* or the *Terrestrial Kingdoms* will continue to live on the earth. LDS members will continue to evangelize the living and perform ordinances for the dead.

At the Last Judgment, Jesus will consign each soul to one of three degrees of glory, called heavenly kingdoms.

The highest heavenly kingdom is the Celestial Kingdom, the permanent residence of God the Father and Jesus Christ. This location is for those who have accepted Jesus Christ and have received all saving ordinances, either as a mortal or by proxy.[8] If a child dies at age eight or younger, they automatically go to this kingdom. Individuals receive a new name there and they will continue to progress spiritually. Eventually they will become gods and goddesses and have spirit children.

The Terrestrial Kingdom or the second highest heaven is a place of glory in Christ's presence, but not the "Fullness of the Father." This location is for righteous people who refuse to accept the saving ordinances and for those who fail to keep covenant commitments.[9] These individuals lived respectable lives but were "blinded by the craftiness of men" and rejected the fullness of the Mormon Gospel in life. The Terrestrial Kingdom also includes persons who received the Gospel in the spirit world and those who were valiant in the testimony of Jesus."[10]

The lowest heaven is the *Telestial Kingdom*. This location is for those who "received not the gospel of Christ, nor the testimony of Jesus."[11] It includes

---

[7] End time events will occur mostly in North America. This highlights the fact that the LDS sees a special place in the plan of God for the North American continent because of its freedom of religion. Joseph Smith, Jr. believed that Jackson County, Missouri was the original location of the Garden of Eden and will be the future location of the New Jerusalem.

[8] Mormons believe that the Celestial Kingdom is the third heaven referenced by Paul in 2 Corinthians 12:2.

[9] Mormons believe that the Terrestrial Kingdom is referred to in 1 Corinthians 15:40-41.

[10] Joseph Smith, Jr., *The Doctrine and Covenants of the Church of Jesus Christ of the Latter-day Saints Doctrine and Covenants* 76 (Whitefish, MT: Kessinger Publishing, LCC, 2006), 74-79 (Hereafter *Doctrine and Covenants*).

[11] *Doctrine and Covenants* 76:82.

most humans since the time of Adam until now, especially "liars, sorcerers, and adulterers, and whoremongers, and whosoever loves and makes a lie."[12]

These individuals will suffer for their sins in hell for 1,000 years during the millennial reign of Christ. Afterward, they will be resurrected with an immortal body and moved into the Telestial Kingdom. The Holy Ghost and beings from the Terrestrial Kingdom will minister to Telestial inhabitants, but God the Father and Jesus Christ will not be there. However, existence in the Telestial Kingdom will be comfortable, not hellish.

One of the most famous aspects of the Latter-day Saints is the way in which most of the faithful live. Mormons have the *Word of Wisdom*, which the church believes was revealed to Smith in 1833 CE. This is a set of guidelines for faithful living. For example, LDS members cannot smoke, drink alcohol and caffeinated beverages.

Another hallmark of Mormon life is the importance of the *Family*, which is headed by a male member. Because it is considered the sacred duty of the faithful to have as many children as possible, cannot be celibate. The church believes that prior to birth souls exist in a spiritual realm. They are brought to earth by the sexual act of humans.

Mormons are discouraged from marrying outside the faith and active homosexuality and adultery are forbidden.

Two significant aspects of Mormon life have been dropped since the founding of the LDS. At one time, the devout were permitted to have more than one wife. This practice has stuck to the church like feathers to tar, even though the church outlawed this practice over 100 years ago.

In recent years, the church has fully accepted black members. Prior to the 1980s CE, blacks were considered inferior to whites and ineligible for membership and ultimately salvation.

On February 13, 1849 CE, Brigham Young announced that blacks were ineligible for Priesthood and hence ineligible for the highest degrees of heaven because they were under the Curse of Cain. Young stated, "The Lord had cursed Cain's seed with blackness and prohibited them from the Priesthood."[13] As a result, Afro-American men could not be ordained as priests and Afro-American men and women could not participate in temple ordinances. In particular, they could not carry out those rituals which were necessary for the highest degrees of salvation.

By revelation, the LDS ended this policy in 1978 CE.[14] Today the LDS has had significant growth in Africa and among Afro-Americans. The church officially opposes racial discrimination.

---

[12] *Doctrine and Covenants* 76:103; Revelation 22:15.
[13] Lester E. Bush, Jr. and Armand L. Mauss, eds., *Neither White Nor Black: Mormon Scholars in a Universal Church* (Salt Lake City: Signature Books, 1984), p. 80.
[14] See "Official Declaration-2" in *Doctrine and Covenants*. See http://scriptures. lds.org/od/2

The Mormon faith teaches and practices self-reliance. According to church tradition, no Mormon ever starved during the depression.

Finally, education on all levels is important for Mormons. The church has its own flagship university (i.e., Brigham Young University). Mormons also stress self-reliance and church aid to the needy. The LDS prides itself with the belief that no Mormon starved during the Great Depression because of these aspects of church life.

The LDS has two ordinances, saving and non-saving ones. All must be performed by designated members of the priesthood. The former are those required for *Exaltation*. They are also linked with one or more covenant that the person receiving the ordinance makes with God, and one or more blessing that God promises to the recipient:

| | |
|---|---|
| • Baptism: | Carried out by immersion for the remission of sins at around eight years of age; re-baptism of excommunicated or disfellowshipped members; carried out in local churches. |
| • Laying on of Hands: | For the gift of the Holy Spirit (confirmation of membership in the Church of Jesus Christ); must be baptized; carried out in churches. |
| • Ordination to the office of the Priesthood: | For both the Aaronic (age 12) and Melchizedek (age 18); for males only; must hold Aaronic prior to the Melchizedek and must be baptized and confirmed; carried out in churches.[15] |
| • The Endowment: | See later section on temple rites. |
| • Celestial Marriage: | See later section on temple rites. |
| • Family Sealings: | See later section on temple rites. |

Non-saving ordinances include:

| | |
|---|---|
| • Sacrament of the Lord's Supper | Held each Sunday in remembrance of the Atonement of Jesus Christ and |

---

[15] See later in this section of this chapter for more information on the Aaronic and Melchizedek Priesthoods.

to renew the covenants made at baptism; carried out in churches.

- The Prayer Circle (True Order of Prayer):    An antiphonic recitation of prayer by participants encircling an altar.

- The Hosanna Shout:    An organized corporate yell of Hosanna at a temple's dedication.

- Shaking the Dust from the Feet:    Given by an elder priesthood member to another for gifting and wisdom.

- Dedication of Graves:    Prayers of consecration for the grave and for comfort for those left behind. If appropriate, the Melchizedek Priest prayers that the burial plot will be maintained until the Resurrection.

- Dedication of Buildings:    Performed after new building is completed and paid for or when extensive remodeling has been carried out.

- Naming and Blessing a Child:    Performed soon after birth; only done once.

- Consecrating Oil:    To prepare oil for other rituals.

- Anointing and Blessing of Sick and Afflicted:    As needed.

- Priesthood Blessing:    As needed.

- Dedication of Land or Country for the Preaching of the Gospel:    Performed before or soon after missionaries begin work in a country; carried out by an apostle.

Mormons have two places to worship, the local church, of which there can be many, and the *Temple*, of which there are few.[16]

---

[16] Local churches can be called wards or branches depending on size. In 2007, there were 27,827 of these. See http://lds.org/conference/talk/display/0,5232,23-1-851-9,00.html

Open to members and non-members alike, worship at local churches resembles worship at non-liturgical churches. These three-hour services usually contain three parts: The Sacrament Meeting, Sunday School, and other Meetings.

One part of the worship is the *Sacrament Meeting*. During this activity, hymns are sung, talks or testimonies are given, prayers are offered, church business is conducted, church ordinances are done (i.e., naming and blessing of children, for example), and the Sacrament is held.

During the Sacrament itself, Aaronic Priesthood members bless the bread which is distributed by deacons. Next, the same priests bless the water which the deacons give out to members. When the elements are blessed the following prayer is said:

O God, the Eternal Father, we ask thee in the name of thy Son, Jesus Christ, to bless and sanctify this bread to the souls of all those who partake of it, that they may eat in remembrance of the body of thy Son, and witness unto thee, O God, the Eternal Father, that they are willing to take upon them the name of thy Son, and always remember him and keep his commandments which he has given them; that they may always have his Spirit to be with them. Amen.

O God, the Eternal Father, we ask thee in the name of thy Son, Jesus Christ, to bless and sanctify this wine to the souls of all those who drink of it, that they may do it in remembrance of the blood of thy Son, which was shed for them; that they may witness unto thee, O God, the Eternal Father, that they do always remember him, that they may have his Spirit to be with them. Amen.[17]

No collection plate is passed around because members tithe personally and separately from the church service.

During the second Sunday activity, Sunday school classes are divided by gender and age. Adult classes can be for the curious non-members (The Investigators), for members (Gospel Essentials, Gospel Doctrine and/or a variety of other topics) and for children.

A third activity on Sunday mornings is attendance at a variety of meetings designed to meet the needs of age and gender. Men attend Aaronic and Melchizedek meetings, women attend the Relief Society and Young Women's meetings, and children under the age of 12, Primary.

Mormons do not use the cross as a symbol of faith, except with military chaplains, who use the symbol on their uniforms. Members feel that they

There are about 146 temples in use or under construction as of January 1, 2009. See http://www.lds.org/temples/chronological/0,11206,1900-1,00.html
[17] *Doctrine and Covenants* 20:75-79.

should focus more on a resurrected Jesus than a dying and suffering Jesus. The absence of crosses in local wards is quite obvious to visitors.[18]

Temples are special places where only devout believers can enter, once the temple is dedicated. A letter of endorsement (i.e., "Temple Recommend") must be held from the local bishop to enter a temple. Upon entering, the faithful change into white robes.

Three major ceremonies are carried out inside temples. Faithful members normally do not say much about the meanings and practices of each. Progression toward exaltation requires participation in these three rituals.

First, there is the *Endowment*. It has an initiatory phase and an instructional and test phase. The former contains instruction, multiple washings and anointing ordinances, putting on a temple garment and the reception of a new name. In the second part, detailed teaching is given on Mormon theology and history. Afterward, the participant is tested on what they have learned. They are also given key words, signs, and tokens to remind them of their new knowledge. As part of the Endowment, the faithful pledge to follow the church's teachings. This ceremony is the basis for the other two.

A second ceremony is *Eternal Marriage* (also called the New and Everlasting Covenant or Celestial Marriage). This is required if the devout wish to reside in the upper realms of exaltation.

The practice of Eternal Marriage is one aspect of the concept of "sealing" in the LDS. Sealing is an ordinance or ritual which cements familial relationships for eternity. It must be done by those with priestly authority and it is normally carried out in temples. Sealings are done for the living as well as in proxy for the dead. If done for the dead, the permanence takes effect in the afterlife.

In this ceremony a husband and wife make pledges to one another and to God and are "sealed" for "now and eternity" not "until death do us part." Church doctrine is not clear about the status of sealed partners in multiple spouse situations (i.e., when a spouse dies and then the living spouse remarries; the church does not permit polygamous relationships). The possibilities are:

- Men and women are sealed and live in eternity with one spouse. Extra spouses will be assigned another spouse in the afterlife to have an eternal marriage.
- Men and women with multiple sealings create plural marriages in life and in the afterlife. Men may have sealings in this life or by proxy in the afterlife. However, women can only do multiple sealings in the afterlife.

---

[18] My teenage son noticed this during a tour of a local ward and temple prior to the latter's dedication.

For eternal marriages to remain in effect in this life, a person must remain a righteous and devout LDS member. If a person remains faithful, but their partner does not, they are promised another partner in the afterlife.

Civilly divorced individuals must have a cancellation of their sealings to seal again.

Children of sealed parents are automatically set for eternity. Children born prior to the sealing or adopted children must undergo a separate ritual for sealing to have the effect of the ordinance. If a sealing is undone, the children's status does not change.

Only worthy LDS members with temple endorsements can witness a couple's sealing in the temple. Non-family members and friends normally wait in the temple waiting room during the ceremony.

The third ceremony Mormons practice in temples is baptizing of dead individuals by living persons (i.e., proxies). This ritual is also called *Baptism for the Dead* (Vicarious Baptism or Proxy Baptism). It is performed so the dead can have the chance to accept the church's teaching in the afterlife. As a result, they can then enter a higher level of Exaltation.[19] Those in the afterlife have the free will to accept or reject this proxy baptism.

To be a proxy, any LDS member, male or female, has to be at least twelve years old. They have to have a current temple recommend. Men must be members of the Aaronic Priesthood. Men are baptized for men and women for women. Baptisms are carried out by immersion. To baptize, a male (no females) must be part of the Melchizedek Priesthood and must have gone through the Endowment Ordinance.

This explains why Mormons have such an interest in genealogy and are one of the best sources for genealogical research.

The Church of Jesus Christ of the Latter-day Saints believes that their church is a *Theocracy* or a church ruled by God himself. It has a hierarchical structure, with clearly defines tasks for each position. Those who have ministries are not elected, but are "called" by someone of a higher authority in the Church; lower positions are not paid for their service. General Authorities, The Quorum of the Twelve, and the First Presidency are paid for their administrative duties, but not as religious clergy.

The global Church of Jesus Christ of the Latter-day Saints has a president, who serves until death. He is advised by two counselors. These three make up the First Presidency. A Quorum of Twelve Apostles advises the First Presidency. These leaders are all seen by the church as prophets, seers, and revelators.

Beyond these are the Presiding Bishopric and the First and Second Quorums of the Seventy. These are all called General Authorities because they supervise the ministry of the church throughout the world.

---

[19] LDS members cite 1 Corinthians 15:29 and John 3:5 to support this practice.

Other church leaders are named Area and Local Authorities because there leadership extends to areas and smaller areas or localities. These include other Quorums of the Seventy, mission presidents, stake presidents, bishops, and other priesthood quorum presidents.

The church has no salaried ministry. Some non-clerical employees are paid a stipend. For example, General Authorities who show a need receive stipends from the church. Area and local authorities are unpaid and carry on their routine occupations while acting as leaders. Members of the priesthoods are generally unpaid. LDS missionaries are self-supporting or are supported by families, local congregations, or the Church as a whole.

The *Aaronic* and *Melchizedek Priesthoods* are given to male members age 12 and older who follow the church's codes of morality. The priesthoods are received by ordination, which occurs when other priesthood holders lay hands on the one being ordained.

The LDS priesthood has two levels, the lower or Aaronic (i.e., Levitical) and the higher or Melchizedek (also called The High Priesthood of the Holy Order of God, The Holy Priesthood, after the Holy Order of God, High Priesthood or The Holy Priesthood, After the Order of the Son of God). Within each there are different levels. The former includes deacon, teacher, priest, and bishop. The latter has elder, high priest, patriarch, seventy, and apostle.

The earliest age for a young man to join the Aaronic Priesthood is around age 12. He normally moves to the Melchizedek Priesthood around age 18. The main job of the Aaronic Priesthood is to train, lead and provide services for adolescent boys and new converts.

The main purpose of the Melchizedek Priesthood is to give fathers and husbands the authority to confer priesthood blessings of healing, comfort, counsel, and strength to their families. Many LDS fathers give a priesthood blessing to their children at the beginning of a new school year or before an important life event such as marriage. Each Melchizedek priesthood bearer, regardless of priesthood office, is encouraged to give priesthood blessings when asked. Besides the priesthood blessings, Melchizedek priests serve the Church in a variety of leadership positions.

A prominent feature of the LDS is its missionary work. All members are encouraged to do full-time or part-time missions at their own expense. Unmarried men ages 19 to 25 are especially encouraged to spend 2 years in full-time missions work. Young women are encouraged to spend an 18 month stint. Missionaries are generally self-supporting or supported by family, friends, or local wards. In June 2007 CE, the church reported its one millionth full-time missionary since the community's founding in 1830 CE.[20]

---

[20] Press Release, LDS Church, "One Million Missionaries, Thirteen Million Members," June 25, 2007.

## The Community of Christ (RLDS)

The RLDS is the second largest group within Mormon Restorationism with approximately 250,000 members. The community traces its roots back to the experience and teachings of Joseph Smith in 1830 CE and says it is a "reorganization" of those things in 1860 CE. From 1872-2001 CE, its name was the Reorganized Church of Jesus Christ of Latter Day Saints. In 2001 CE, the church renamed itself the *Community of Christ*. The RLDS owns Graceland University and Community of Christ Seminary on the Graceland campus.[21]

Since 1844 CE, the doctrines and practices of the RLDS have evolved and constantly changed. The Bible is used in public and private worship. While it uses a variety of translations, including the *Revised Standard Version*, the church uses Joseph Smith's translation of the *King James Version* of the Bible called either the *Inspired Version of the Bible* (IV) or the *Joseph Smith Translation of the Bible* (JST). This version contains doctrines and practices Smith thought had been deleted from the Bible, inspired commentary by Smith and harmonizations of Smith's doctrines with the Bible.

Like in other LDS communities, extra books are also seen as scripture. Affirmation Nine of the Community's "Scripture in the Community of Christ" states:

With other Christians, we affirm the Bible as the foundational scripture for the church. In addition, the Community of Christ uses the *Book of Mormon* and the *Doctrine and Covenants* as scripture. We do not use these sacred writings to replace the witness of the Bible or improve upon it, but because they confirm its message that Jesus Christ is the Living Word of God We have heard Christ speak in all three books of scripture, and bear witness that he is "alive forever and ever." (Revelation 1:18)[22]

The Community of Christ's version of *Doctrine and Covenants* is an ever-growing collection of inspired documents given through the prophet-presidents of the Community of Christ. The church does not use *The Pearl of Great Price.*

The concept of *Zion* is very important to the RLDS. The term is not associated with a specific place, but with an attitude and approach to a way of life. The church's website says, "The "cause of Zion" expresses our commitment to pursuing God's kingdom through the establishment of Christ-centered communities in families, congregations, neighborhoods, cities, and throughout the world."[23]

---

[21] The oldest and main campus of Graceland University is located in Lamoni, Iowa. The seminary is found at the Independence, Missouri campus.

[22] "Preface of the Book of Mormon," *Doctrine and Covenants* 76: 3g.

[23] http://www.cofchrist.org/ourfaith/faith-beliefs.asp

The Community of Christ believes in continuing revelation and the significant role of prophets. That is, God speaks today just as he did in ancient times and with equal authority.

The Community of Christ emphasizes *Peace* and *Justice*. As a "peace and justice church," the Independence Temple is "dedicated to the pursuit of peace."[24] Each day of the year at 1:30 P.M. Central Time, the faithful convene a Daily Prayer for Peace in the Independence Temple. Each Friday at noon Eastern Time a Friday Prayer for Peace meets at the Community of Christ Spiritual Formation Center section of the Kirkland Temple Complex. In addition, the annual Community of Christ International Peace Award has been given since 1993 CE (except 1996).

The church uses a three-lectionary cycle (i.e., the *Revised Common Lectionary*) based on the one used by other Christians. The RLDS lectionary also includes readings from the *Book of Mormon* and *Doctrine and Covenants*. Its English-language hymnal is called *Hymns of the Saints*, published in 1981 CE.

The Community of Christ practices eight sacraments: Baptism, Confirmation (which is open to all), Blessing of Children, The Lord's Supper, Marriage, Administration to the Sick, Ordination, and Evangelist's Blessing. The Laying on of Hands is used in Confirmation, Ordination, Blessing of children, Administration and Evangelist's Blessing. Unlike their LDS counterpart, the Community of Christ does not practice baptism for the dead.

The church owns the *Kirkland Temple* in Kirkland, Missouri and the Independence, Missouri Temple. The former was dedicated in 1836 CE and the latter in 1994 CE. Temple worship has no private ceremonies and is open to everyone. The sacraments performed there are Communion, Laying on of Hands for the Sick, and Ordination.

The Community of Christ considers Joseph Smith III to have been the only legitimate prophet to succeed his father as opposed to the LDS which believes that a non-family member could succeed Joseph Smith, Jr.

Church leadership is composed of the one in ten church members who hold the priesthood office. These are mostly unpaid, bi-vocational ministers. There is a small cadre of professional ministers, who are paid salaries. These may be local pastors or administrators, financial officers, or missionaries.

The main task of all Priesthood members is to preach the gospel or "good news" of Jesus Christ. On the congregational level, priesthood members (ordained ministers) and the laity (non-ordained) direct all church ministries. In most congregations the pastor(s) and other elected and/or appointed officials serve without salary. In 1984 CE, women were given the power to hold the priesthood.

Other church officers (all open to women) include:

- The First Presidency: This three member group of president and two counselors presides

---

[24] *Doctrine and Covenants* 156:5.

over the international church. It is composed of the president and two counselors.

- Prophet or Prophet-President:

The President of the church. He brings inspired messages or documents to the church, which the church has to approve during its annual world conferences if the text is to be added to the collection of inspired scriptures.

- Presiding Bishopric:

The Presiding Bishop and two counselors serve as the financial officers of the international church.

- Council of Twelve Apostles:

These 12 priests are called by witnesses and are assigned by the First Presidency. They are responsible for church expansion and direct the geographic divisions of the church.

- Order of Evangelists:

This person directs the church's counseling, crisis, and evangelistic ministries.

- Quorum of High Priests:

This person presides over a group of experienced, mature ministers who provide a wide array of ministry and often hold leadership positions in the church.

- Office of Seventy:

This group assists with missionary work. There are seven Presidents of Seventy, each with a quorum or group of missionaries in specific geographic areas.

## The Fundamentalist Church of Jesus Christ of Latter Day Saints (FLDS)

This branch of Mormon Restorationism has been featured prominently in recent news reports because of events in 2008 CE in Texas where 416 children of church members were removed from the religious compound for charges of child abuse. Later, the Texas Supreme Court ordered the children be returned.[25]

The FLDS was founded in 1935 CE by two excommunicated LDS members, *John Y. Barlow* and *John White Musser*, primarily over the issue of *polygamy.*[26] This group wished to continue this practice, whereas the LDS had dropped the practice in 1890 CE when Church President *Wilfred Woodruff* suspended the blessing of plural marriages just prior to Utah assuming statehood. Woodruff's action was called *The Great Accommodation.*[27]

The FLDS considers itself to be the only true descendants of Joseph Smith and his original church. It calls its members "Original Mormons" or "Fundamentalist Mormons."

Currently, the Church has approximately 10,000 members, located in Hildale, Utah; Colorado City, Arizona; Eldorado, Texas; Westcliffe, Colorado; Mancos, Colorado; Creston and Bountiful, British Columbia and Pringle, South Dakota. Since 2004 CE, its headquarters has been found in Eldorado, Texas at *Yearning for Zion Ranch*. By 2008 CE, the group had constructed 36 buildings and a temple on their ranch.

Members of the FLDS have owned machine shops that have sold airplane parts to the United States government. From 1999-2007 CE, these sales have totaled 1.7 million dollars.

FLDS members believe that Brigham Young once visited Hildale and Colorado City and stated, "This is the right place (and it) will someday be the head not the tail of the church."[28]

---

[25] On April 3, 2008 CE a sixteen year-old pregnant woman, a FLDS member, contacted an abuse hotline on several occasions and claimed to have been abused by her husband, who was 49-50 years of age. Acting on her calls, Texas Protective Services raided the facility and removed 183 people (97 girls and 40 boys) by April 5. On April 6, the LDS issued a statement saying that they were not connected to the FLDS and had given up polygamy in 1890 CE. By April 6, 60 adults and 159 children had been removed and an arrest warrant was issued for Dale Barlow, the man accused of fathering the 16 year old woman's child. By April 15, the number of children removed was 416 (infants to seventeen-year-olds). By April 27, the number had grown to 467. These children were separated from their mothers and placed in foster care facilities in Texas. On May 8, 48 mothers filed a lawsuit to have their children returned, saying that Texas Protective Services did not have enough evidence to justify their actions. On Thursday, May 29, the Texas Supreme Court decided that there was not enough evidence to remove the children from the FLDS compound. They declared that the children should be returned as soon as possible.

[26] The practice in question was really polygyny not polygamy. Polygyny is the practice of one man having more than one wife. Polygamy is a broader term and refers to any person having more than one spouse at the same time.

[27] The Woodruff Manifesto (1890 CE).

[28] See "About the Fundamentalist Church of Jesus Christ of Latter Day Saints" at http://www.religioustolerance.org/flds.htm

Succeeding leaders have included *Rulon Jeffs* (1986-2002 CE) and his son, *Warren Jeffs* (2002-2007 CE). In May 2006 CE, Jeffs was put on the FBI's "Ten Most-Wanted List." Later in 2006, he was arrested and was found guilty of two counts of rape as an accomplice. Today, Jeffs is serving a ten-year term at the Utah State Prison. At this point, it is unsure who the real leader of this community is.

The FLDS adheres to the accepted beliefs and practices of Mormon Restorationism. However, some distinctive beliefs of the FLDS include:

- Plural Marriage: A man must have more than one wife to attain the highest level of exaltation.

- Three Wives Teaching: The FLDS teaches that a man should have a minimum of three wives to attain the highest degree of exaltation. Women must be married to a man with at least two other wives.

- Placement Marriage: By revelation to the leader of the church, who is considered a prophet, a woman of marriageable age is assigned to a husband.

- Law of Placing: The prophet chooses to give wives to or take wives from their husbands according to the men's worthiness.

- The Patriarchal Doctrine: A wife must be subordinate to her husband.

- Dress: Women do not cut their hair short or wear makeup, trousers, or skirts above the knee. They normally wear full-length "prairie dresses," which are solid color and are homemade. Their hair is coiffed. Men wear plain clothes, usually long-sleeved collared shirt and full-length trousers.

- Property Ownership: The church owns all official property and most of the businesses controlled by members. In 2006 CE, the property was worth 100 million dollars.

- Home Schooling:

  All children are homeschooled by order of the prophet.

- Racial Views:

  The Southern Law Poverty Center has put the FLDS on its hate group list because condemns interracial relationships. Jeffs said that the devil has been able to bring evil into the world through the black race.[29]

## SEE WHAT YOU KNOW ABOUT JOSEPH SMITH AND MORMON RESTORATIONISM

1. Identify and describe four beliefs.

2. Identify and describe three characteristics of lifestyle.

---

[29] "In His Own Words," Intelligence Report (Montgomery: Southern Poverty Law Center (Spring 2005) or at http://www.splcenter.org/intel/intelreport/article.jsp?sid =342

3. Identify and describe four characteristics of ceremonies.

4. Identify and describe three characteristics of institutions.

# CHAPTER XVII
✠
# OTHER PROTESTANT CHURCH, SECT, AND CULT COMMUNITIES

Here are some other communities that are typically part of the church, sect, cult discussion.

### Jehovah's Witnesses

The official name of the Jehovah's Witnesses is the Watchtower Bible and Tract Society. The emphasis on *Jehovah* comes from their teaching that Isaiah 43:12 states that God is called by this name.

The group has its own Bible translation, *The New World Translation* (1961). They believe that their translation corrects the errors of all other translations of the Bible.[1]

Jehovah's Witnesses do not believe in the Trinity. Instead they teach that there is one God, Jehovah, who had a son named Jesus, the first of all his creations and a human being. Jesus is also named the Archangel Michael. Jesus was only a man when he died on a stake instead of a cross and when he rose from the dead. At that time, Jehovah made him higher than angels in a spirit body, while his dead body remained in the grave. His body has disappeared. It either has dissolved or been hidden. Jesus died to pay a ransom for all humans to save them from life's end at physical death and to give them eternal life. The Holy Spirit is an active, impersonal force. Salvation comes from accepting the group's teachings and by an active life of service to Jeho-

---

[1] For example *The New World Translation* translates John 1:1, "In the beginning was the Word. The Word was with God and the Word was a god." This version teaches that Jesus was godlike, but not divine. Greek scholars typically translate the text, "In the beginning was the Word, The Word was with God and the Word was God." This translation teaches that Jesus was God.

vah. This involves door-to-door evangelism, which includes personal testi-mony and the passing out of the group's literature.

Only a limited number of Witnesses (*144,000*) will live with God after death; the rest will live in peace and harmony on a new earth. Those that do not go either place, cease to exist.[2] The community does not believe that the damned go to hell.

For this movement, Satan's most influential allies are government, the business community and the church. They do not believe that the higher powers mentioned in Romans 13 are civil authorities, but instead are Jehovah and Christ Jesus.

Jehovah's Witnesses do not involve themselves in the political process. Group members do not run for office, serve in the military, salute the flag, or sing the national anthem. They do not celebrate birthdays or Christmas. The Witnesses contend that Jesus was born around October 1.

The faithful do not take *Blood Transfusions* because blood is sacred and is life on its most fundamental level in Jehovah's eyes. Blood should not be eaten or transfused and blood should be disposed of once it leaves the hu-man body.[3] The Jehovah's Witnesses community teaches that a person can-not use transfused blood in emergencies and if they do, they can be disfel-lowshipped or disassociated (i.e., shunned).

Jehovah's Witnesses do not regard themselves as a church, but rather as a group of *Bible Students* and publishers of God's word.

The movement calls its buildings *Kingdom Halls* not churches. Many of these facilities are built by volunteers from the community. Each congrega-tion meets at least twice a week (Sunday morning and Midweek).

The Sunday morning meeting normally lasts an hour and 45 minutes and includes songs (i.e., Kingdom Songs), prayer, and study. There are two stud-ies: the Public Talk and the Watchtower Study. The former is for non-Jehovah's Witnesses and the latter is for committed members. During the Watchtower Study, Witnesses spend their time in Bible study, using pre-written materials in a question and answer format, which have been provided by the religion's headquarters. A leader asks questions and audiences respond with the printed answers provided.

The Midweek meeting consists of a congregational Bible study, the *Theo-cratic Ministry School* to train "publishers" how to go door-to-door effectively and the Service Meeting to train members to be more efficient in their ministries. Witnesses baptize by immersion and their services allow for testimonies and prayer.

---

[2] Jehovah's Witnesses cite Ecclesiastes 9:5 to support their belief in annihilationalism: "For the living know that they will die, but the dead know nothing, and they have no more reward, for their remembrance is forgotten."
[3] Jehovah's Witnesses cite Genesis 9:3, Leviticus 17:11 and Acts 15:29.

Once a year (similar to the Jewish Passover), believers can attend the *Lord's Evening Meal* (or the "Memorial") normally in their Kingdom Halls. Jehovah's Witnesses contend that this is the only ritual that Jesus commanded to be carried out. A minority of those in attendance at the Memorial receive the bread and wine offered.[4] Communion is taken by those who feel they are part of the 144,000.

The community holds several annual meetings: a Special Assembly Day, a Circuit Assembly, and District Conventions. Circuit assemblies are gatherings of 20 congregations in local areas for 2 or 3 days of meetings. District Conventions are held for about 200 congregations once a year and last for 3 to 5 days. Every fifth year, International Conventions are held in selected cities. These normally last three to four days with visiting delegates from other countries.

Baptism of converts who understand and accept to do Jehovah's will through Jesus Christ are totally immersed at large meetings and not at kingdom halls.

The Movement has a tightly organized hierarchical structure called a *Theocratic Government.* The group is headed by the Governing Body of Jehovah's Witnesses, located in Brooklyn, New York. The governing body is made up of 6 committees which over the work of the community in its 115 branches. District and Circuit Overseers are appointed within each branch to supervise local congregations.

Each congregation is led by locally appointed male elders assisted by ministerial servants. Elders run the congregation by handling the facility, setting meeting times, selecting speakers, conducting meetings, supervising evangelism, and providing for disciplining errant members. Ministerial servants assist elders in the routine governance of the Kingdom Hall.

### The Christian Identity Movement

The term Christian Identity refers to the member's belief that the whites are God's chosen people. Citing biblical support, the Christian Identity Movement teaches the superiority of whites over all non-whites and non-Protestants.

Origins of this view of racial superiority can be found in the writings of John Wilson and his book, *Lectures on Our Israelitish Origins* (1840). Wilson wrote that the "ten lost tribes of Israel" merged into the pagan cultures of Europe, especially Britain after the 8th century. Hence, Anglo-Saxons were inheritors of the promises made to Israel in the Old Testament. *Anglo-Israelism* was not originally anti-Semitic. Jews along with Anglo-Saxons were God's chosen ones.

---

[4] In 2008, 9,986 out of 17,790,631 took the bread and wine. See *Yearbook of Jehovah's Witnesses 2009* (New York: Watch Tower and Tract Society of Pennsylvania, 2009), p. 31.

By the 1920s CE, some advocates of this doctrine added *Anti-Semitism* to Anglo-Israelism. Examples include Henry Ford and his media consultant William Cameron. Cameron ran some articles on "The International Jew" in Ford's Dearborn *Independent* in 1920 CE. This series was based on "The Protocols of the Learned Elders of Zion," a fake document that was clearly anti-Semitic. At first, these were required reading at all Ford automotive plants. However, in 1927 CE, Ford denounced Cameron and these writings and closed down the newspaper.

In the late 1930s CE, several meetings held in California brought together the young leaders of the Christian Identity Movement. A newly emerging leader, *Gerald Smith*, was the pivotal force in assembling these leaders. He demanded that all "Zionists" and all Afro-Americans be deported, that all Jewish organizations (which he called Gestapo groups) be forbidden, and later that the United Nations be shut down.

Many of Smith's group went on to launch their own Identity movements. William Gale founded the Posse Comitatus, which argues that there is no governmental power beyond the local sheriff. A member of this group, Gordon Kahl, a tax protester, was killed in a gunfight with authorities in 1983 CE. Dan Gayman, head of the Church of Israel, articulated the "seed line" and "serpent's seed" teachings. *Richard Butler*, founder of the *Aryan Nation*, held annual meetings, the Aryan National Congress. Aryan Nation has an active prison ministry and publishes *The Way*. Countless numbers of people have been touched through its Internet sites, publications, and cable broadcasts.

Christian Identity members claim to be Protestant Christians, who affirm that the Bible is the sole authority for faith and practice. It is unclear what they believe about the Trinity and the atonement, but they most likely have basic Christian teachings. Beyond these, these believers affirm the following:

- Anglo-Israelism: Anglo-Saxons, or more broadly whites, are the chosen people and the contemporary recipients of the promises made to ancient Israelites.

- Pre-Adamite Theory: Whites are the true descendants of Adam. People of other races come from human beings created before Adam. They are called the "beasts of the earth." Asians and Africans are included.

- Serpent's Seed Doctrine: Cain was the offspring of Eve and Satan (the serpent). Jews, "the mongrels," come from the combination of Cain and his descendents and the Pre-Adamites. Jews are the result of Eve's original sin. This is called the Two Seeds Doctrine.

- Armageddon as an Immanent Race War:

The conflict between a woman's seed and the serpent's seed (Genesis 3:15) is really about a future fight between whites and non-whites, especially the Jews. Jews dominate the world, especially the United Nations, the United States government, and all major social organizations. Resistance by whites to Jewish dominance of the world will lead to Armageddon. North America is the new promised land and the location of the final stand between whites and non-whites.

Paramilitary training is stressed in preparation for the end-time battle where Christ and all faithful whites will ultimately triumph. Christian Identity churches are non-liturgical and generally practice two ordinances: believers' baptism and the Lord's Supper.

The Christian Identity Movement is small in number and lacks central organization and leadership. The movement's name is an umbrella term for a variety of independent churches, which hold that the Bible is the sole authority for faith and practice. Some churches in this movement include:

- Kingdom Identity Ministries
- The Church of Jesus Christ Christian/Aryan Nation (CJCC/AN)
- The Covenant, the Sword, and the Arm of the Lord (CSA)

### Christian Naturism

*Christian Nudism* (or Naturism) is a movement composed of believers who practice nudism or naturism. This group has its origin in the secular nudist movement. The Christian version began with *Reverend Ilsley Boone*. Boone ("Uncle Danny" with affection or "The Dictator" with disdain) was a charismatic speaker and powerful organizer. He is considered the founder of the major American nudist organization, The American Association for Nude Recreation (which has 50,000 registered members and 267 affiliated clubs and resorts), then called the American Sunbathing Association. In 1933 CE,

Boone started to publish the first nudist magazine in the U.S., *The Nudist*, and later, *Sunshine & Health*.[5]

Today Christian Nudists can be found in almost all branches and denominations of Christianity.[6] They have founded organizations, have websites, and host annual gatherings of believing naturists.[7]

No one knows exactly how many Christian Naturists actually exist. There are several Christian nudist Yahoo discussion groups and websites.[8] The Nudist Fig Leaf Forum has about 600 subscribers.[9]

Christian Naturists find no conflict between the teachings of the Bible and lives lived without any clothing. They find links between nudity and the Bible in Paul Bowman's self-published book, *Nakedness and the Bible*.[10]

---

[5] Even with the genitals airbrushed, the U.S. Postal Service made the decision that the materials were obscene and could not be mailed through the U.S. system. This issue was dealt with all the way to the Supreme Court where the Rev. Boone eventually won the right to distribute nudist materials through the U.S. mails. This victory opened the door for not only legitimate nudist magazines and materials, but also for less reputable materials and, eventually, Hugh Hefner's *Playboy* empire.

[6] An online poll of 1,069 active users of the naturist-christians.org website found the following results:

20.39%   Non-Denominational
18.71%   Roman Catholic/Orthodox
15.53%   Baptist
12.63%   Jewish
10.01%   Other
6.45%   Pentecostal/Charismatic
5.24%   Lutheran
5.00% or less   Agnostic/Atheist, Episcopal/Anglican, Methodist, Presbyterian, Mormon

[7] The logo of one website, christian-naturism.com, features a very happy nude family, parents and children, holding hands with the slogans, "Discover the Joy, Experience the Freedom and Because Your Best Sunday Suit is the One God Gave You."

Examples of discussion groups include: Naturist-Christians-org (4461 members), Christian_Teen_Naturist (831 members), Colorado_Christian_Naturist (62 members), NJChristian-Nudist (42 members), christian_naturist_singles (5 members), Christian-Naturist-Australia (20 members) and Brisbane_Christian_Naturists (16 members).

Examples of websites include: http://naturist.r2bw.com/home.htm, http://reject shame.r2bw.com/, and http://www.experiencegrace.com/

[9] Figleafforum.com

[10] Chapters include: Actual Nakedness in the Bible, Allegorical Nakedness in the Bible, Implied Nakedness in the Bible, Clothing during Bible Times, Lust and Nakedness, Passages used to Oppose Nakedness that do not mention nakedness, and an Appendix called Good Nakedness by Pastor Jeff Bowman (not Paul Bowman).

In 2005 CE, a statement of faith was adopted by 86% of participants on a major Naturist Christian website. Besides affirmations on the Bible, Trinity, the Virgin Birth, and the Resurrection of Jesus, the statement makes a few related to nudism:

- We believe that all people are divinely created in God's own image, and their unclothed forms are covered and blessed in his righteousness.

- We believe that the naked human form is inherently good and wholesome.[11]

Naturists hold several other convictions. While Naturism may refer to nature worship, this is not the case for Christian Naturists. Christian Naturists understand nature worship to be idolatry. The creator is to be worshipped, not creation.

The Bible is the Word of God and it is full of references that place nudity in a positive light and offer encouragement to be clothes-free.[12] The Bible also contains passages that demonstrate that nudity is inappropriate on certain occasions and in certain situations.[13]

Nudity and sexuality do not go together and any inappropriate sexual conduct (including lust) goes against the Bible's teachings. Naturists have very strict rules for appropriate sexual conduct based on biblical interpretation.[14]

---

[11] http://www.naturist-christians.org/modules.php?name=Statement_of_Faith

[12] Some biblical passages cited by Naturists include: Genesis 2:25, 3:11 (God never told Adam and Eve they were naked); Genesis 1:31 (all is good, even the naked human); Micah 1:8, 1 Samuel 19:23-24 and Isaiah 20:2-4 (Prophets preach naked); John 19:23 (Jesus hung on the cross naked). According to Naturists, ancient crucifixions were usually done with the victim naked. There is no reason to think that Jesus' crucifixion was done differently. Any depictions of him with clothes on the cross are a concession to modern-day clothed society.

[13] Nudists argue that the Bible rejects human nudity when it involves direct sin (orgies, Paganism, or temple prostitution).

[14] According to the cnvillage.org website in reference to summer convocations, the following statement is made: "There is much confusion in our culture and especially within Christendom regarding the nature and morality of nudity. Many believe that nudity and sexual misconduct go hand in hand. However, we strongly affirm that nudism is not about sex. Furthermore, because of the prevalent misunderstanding regarding the relationship between nudity and sex, it is especially important that we take a very firm stance regarding sexual conduct at all CNC events. This is important for those who attend our events and for those who would question our motives for embracing nudism. This is our stance:

- Sexual expression between married couples is private and not for public display. Couples are asked to limit themselves to simple expressions of affection when in public.

Although "openness" and "loving others as they are" are common beliefs within Christianity, these are especially emphasized in Christian Naturism through *Body Acceptance* (the acceptance of everyone just as they are).

Finally, believers are called to imitate Jesus, to follow God's pattern for living as found in the Bible, and to live in a right relationship with God as Adam and Eve did in the Garden. This includes the freedom to be naked and unashamed before Him and others.

Examples of Christian Naturist activities abound. Nudist Resort and Camp grounds have worship services. Non-denominational services are the most universal among Protestant Naturists. Often someone's home or a portion of a secular nudist resort is used. Several resorts have chapels.

Annual Christian nudist convocations are held regionally during the summer months at a naturist resort. According to the Christian Nudist Convocation website, Christian Convocations were planned for Tennessee, Missouri, and Texas during the summer of 2008 CE and others were planned for 2009 CE.[15] The website makes it clear that these will be Christian, Nudist Convocations with a special emphasis on families. Non-Christians are welcome.

---

- Sexual activity between unmarried couples is contrary to God's Word and will not be condoned by CNC.

- Suggestive comments, innuendoes and jokes are contrary to our ideals and are not appropriate.

- "Swinging" is against God's moral law and will not be tolerated.

- Adults are not to spend time alone with children that are not their own except by the express permission of the parents/guardians.

Violations of the standards of sexual conduct will be considered by a committee of the CNC leadership team and the resort owners in order to determine an appropriate response. Action will only be taken when violations can be affirmed by two or more witnesses. Zero-tolerance will be the guiding standard for our decisions. Any suspected violations of these standards are to be reported to the CNC event leadership team for review and/or action. It is our hope and prayer that all who attend the CNC events will exhibit the character of Christ in all circumstances. We trust that our collective agreement to support this policy statement will ensure that everyone in attendance will have a positive and God honoring experience at the gathering. We thank you in advance for your cooperation."

[15] See http://www.christiannc.com/ This website states that the purpose of the Christian Nudist Convocation is threefold: They "seek to call together Christian Naturists for fellowship while challenging them to be faithful in their service to our Lord"; they "want to equip believers with training and knowledge so that they can effectively impact the naturist community with the Gospel of Jesus Christ"; and they "are also dedicated to educating and serving the Christian Naturist community so that we can be a voice of truth regarding biblical purity and chaste nudity within the greater Christian community."

In 1994 CE, the Fig Leaf Forum was launched as a printed publication. In 1999 CE, a website was launched. Fig Leaf Forum has grown to be one of the best sources available for information and opinion about Christian involvement in social nudism. The Fig Leaf Forum provides fellowship and encouragement for Bible-believing Christian naturists from all across the nation.

The website contains one portion called "The Good News." In this section, a statement affirming personal nudity is given ("As a Christian nudist, I declare that I am not ashamed of my nakedness. My body is the good creation of God, made in His image and likeness" (Genesis 1.26-27).

The website states that the more important statements follow. These include a basic call to salvation in Jesus Christ. The Forum values reverence for God and the human body, chastity, responsibility, and respect for those who are not nudists. It affirms family oriented social nudism and upholds traditional Christian marriage (between one man and one woman) and traditional Christian sexual morality (sex in heterosexual marriage only). The Forum recognizes the role that Christians play within the larger nudist community (through evangelism and supporting traditional morality).

Subscribers to the Fig Leaf Forum are encouraged to submit material for publication. Over the years a steadily growing readership has contributed a wide variety of informative and thought-provoking articles, testimonies of faith, accounts of interesting experiences, fiction, poetry, letters to the editor, and more. Along with original material written by subscribers, the newsletter occasionally features excerpts of interest to Christian nudists from books, magazines, and newspapers. Evangelical authors and materials are widely cited (i.e., *The Life Application Bible*, Reverend Charles Swindoll, and William Barclay's Commentaries).

### Seventh-day Adventism

This international movement of over 15 million members began in the 19th century CE after an event called the *Great Disappointment*. Prior to the Civil War, some Christians came to believe in the immediate return of Christ. Dates were established and some even sold their possessions and changed into white robes to wait for Christ's return. When Jesus did not appear on October 22, 1844 CE, the Great Disappointment happened. Some Christians returned to everyday life, while others recanted their faith.

*Ellen G. White* (1827-1915 CE) came to a very different conclusion. Through a series of trances, she became convinced that Christ had only partially returned to earth because Christians had not obeyed the Bible's teachings, in particular the Old Testament.[16]

---

[16] In her lifetime, White had over 2,000 visions and dreams. They varied in length from less than a minute to four hours.

The Seventh-day Adventist Church has always considered White's teachings significant, but not equal to the Bible. According to official documents, "The writings of Ellen White are not a substitute for Scripture. They cannot be placed on the same level. The Holy Scriptures stand alone, the unique standard by which her and all other writings must be judged and to which they must be subject"[17] Yet, as Ellen White herself noted, "The fact that God has revealed His will to men through His Word, has not rendered needless the continued presence and guiding of the Holy Spirit. On the contrary, the Spirit was promised by our Saviour to open the Word to His servants, to illuminate and apply its teachings."[18] Seventh-day Adventists believe most of the teachings of traditional Protestantism and yet they have some distinctive teachings. These include:

| | |
|---|---|
| • Law: | The law of God is embodied in the Ten Commandments, which continue to be binding on Christians. |
| • Sabbath: | The Sabbath should be carried on the seventh day of the week (i.e., from Friday sunset to Saturday sunset). |
| • Second Coming and End Times: | Jesus Christ will visibly return to earth after a "time of trouble," during which the Sabbath will become a worldwide test. The second coming will be followed by a millennial reign of saints in heaven. These saints will reside with God in heaven for eternity. |
| • Holistic Human Nature: | Humans are an indivisible unity of body, soul, mind, and spirit. They do not possess an immortal soul and death prior to the final judgment is an unconscious sleep (i.e., *Soul Sleep*). |
| • Conditional Immortality: | After the Final Judgment, the wicked will not suffer eternal torment in hell, but instead will be permanently destroyed (i.e., *Annihilationism*). |

---

[17] Seventh-day Adventists Believe . . . , Ministerial Association, General Conference of Seventh-day Adventists, Washington D.C., 1988, p. 227.
[18] White, Ellen G. *The Great Controversy Between Christ and Satan: The Conflict of the Ages in the Christian Dispensation* (Mountain View, CA: Pacific Press Publishing Association, 1888), p. VII.

- Great Controversy: Humanity is involved in a *Great Controversy* between Jesus and Satan. This is an elaboration on the common Christian belief that evil began in heaven when an angelic being, Lucifer, rebelled against the law of God.

- Heavenly Sanctuary: At his ascension, Jesus Christ launched an atoning ministry in the *Heavenly Sanctuary*. In 1844 CE, he began to cleanse the heavenly sanctuary in fulfillment of the Day of Atonement.

- Investigative Judgment: A judgment of professed Christians began in 1844 CE, in which the books recording each human's activities are examined for the universe to see. This judgment will declare who is saved and will vindicate the justice of God.

- Remnant: At time's end, there will be a remnant who keep God's commandments and have the testimony of Jesus.

Since the 1860s CE, the Seventh-day Adventist Church has emphasized healthy living. Many followers practice vegetarianism and Kosher laws. This means that members should not use pork, shellfish, and other unclean foods. Adventists also refrain from alcohol, tobacco, illegal drugs, and some avoid coffee and any caffeine.

The Seventh-day Adventists Church had a profound impact on the development of breakfast cereals. John Harvey Kellogg was an early member and his brother William founded the *Kellogg* Company.

Major initiatives by Seventh-day Adventism are education (with over 7,442 schools, colleges, and universities, 1,480,000 million students and 75,000 teachers) and medical care (over 500 health care facilities worldwide and in the United States, 37 hospitals, 6,000 beds, 43,000 employees and cares for about 4 million patients annually).[19]

---

[19] For education statistics, see http://education.gc.adventist.org/ For medical statistics, see http://www.adventisthealthsystem.com/Home/AboutAHS/tabid/55/De-

For Seventh-day Adventists, practicing the *Sabbath* from Friday at sunset to sunset Saturday is probably the group's most notable practice. During this period of time, believers avoid secular employment, although medical and relief work is allowed. Adventists also refrain from shopping, sport activities, and other forms of leisure activity. Church services are held on Saturday morning. Some Adventists gather on Friday nights to hold Vespers or "Opening the Sabbath" and "Closing the Sabbath" services are held on Saturday night.

The major worship service occurs on Saturday morning and begins with "Sabbath School." Most Adventists use denominational *Sabbath School Lessons*. After Sabbath School, the main service is held and follows a non-liturgical format with the central feature being the sermon. The service also includes hymn singing, prayers, collecting money, and scripture readings.[20]

The church practices the two ordinances of believers' baptism and the Lord's Supper. Communion is open to any Christian. It begins with foot washing known as the "Ordinance of Humility," traditionally divided by gender in separate rooms (i.e., some Adventists carry out this ordinance by married couples and family units). After this, unfermented grape juice and unleavened bread are used.

The organizational structure of the Seventh-day Church is connectional with many levels of organization. The term conference is used for several levels.

Membership in the local church is made up of baptized Adventists, all with voting powers.

Positioned above the local church is the local conference or local mission. This is an association of churches within a state, province, or territory. It appoints ministers, owns church land and handles the payment of ministers and the distribution of tithes.

The next level higher is the union conference or union mission, which is comprised of a number of local conferences within a larger territory.

The general conference runs the church and consists of 13 divisions by geographic locations. It has the final say in all matters. A president heads the general conference.

Leadership in the local church is composed of lay elders and deacons, elected by business meetings. These individuals handle the administrative functions of the church and if necessary, carry out religious duties. Deacons make sure that local churches run well and maintain church property. Pastors or ministers are assigned by local conferences and serve churches.

Women played a significant role in the leadership of the early Seventh-day Adventist Movement and continue to do so. They serve as pastors, religion professors, Bible teachers, Bible instructors (workers), and in adminis-

---

fault.aspx

[20] Tithes are collected on the local level and passed on to the overall church.

trative positions on conference, union, division, and General Conference levels.

## SEE WHAT YOU KNOW ABOUT PROTESTANT DIVISIONS— CHURCH, SECT, AND CULT

1. Identify and describe four beliefs.

2. Identify and describe three characteristics of lifestyle.

3. Identify and describe four characteristics of ceremonies.

4. Identify and describe three characteristics of institutions.

CHAPTER XVIII
✠
PROTESTANT DIVISIONS:
THE FIVE UMBRELLA TERMS


*Five Umbrella Terms*
The last way to group Protestants is to divide the movement using five umbrella terms and then associate specific denominations with each term based on observable characteristics.

- Anglican/Episcopal
- Methodist
- Presbyterian/Reformed
- Baptist
- Lutheran

*Anglican/Episcopal*
This umbrella term refers to those churches:

- With historical connections to the Church of England
- With similar beliefs, worship styles, and structures to the Church of England
- In communion with the Archbishop of Canterbury

The terms Anglican and Episcopal are interchangeable. Churches may be called either one depending on geographic location.[1] Although the word Anglican has been used since the 16th century CE, its use has become especially

---

[1] In the United States, the largest body is called Episcopalian (TEC), while smaller groups may be called either Anglican or Episcopalian. In many places, the term Anglican is used, such as the Anglican Church of the Sudan.

visible since the 19th century CE. This is when the identity of a global Anglicanism became firmly established.

Some members and non-members maintain that this tradition is a separate and unique version of Christianity different than Eastern, Roman, and Protestant Christianity. This does not hold up because the movement was one of the four founding members of Protestantism and has all the hallmarks of Protestantism.[2]

Several key terms mark this group:

- Church of England: The "Mother Church" of Anglicanism.

- Anglican: A term derived from the English church; now used as a name for the global community and for churches.

- Episcopal: A term derived from the Greek word for bishop; used as a name by some churches.

- Anglican Church of North America (ACNA): A name for the newly emerging Anglican community in North America outside of the Episcopal church.

- *Book of Common Prayer:* The main book of services for the global Anglican community.

- Archbishop of Canterbury: The leader of the worldwide Anglican community.

- The Episcopal Church (TEC): The name for the largest and oldest Anglican church in North America.

- Churchmanship: High, Broad, and Low church theological approaches.

- The Windsor Report: The Anglican Communion's reaction to the recent crisis triggered by the 2003 CE ordination of Gene Robinson, an American bishop, who is a practicing homosexual.

---

[2] See the "Beliefs and Practices" section of Chapter Six.

Anglican churches contain a mix of Protestant and Roman Catholic elements and are considered *Protestant in Belief and Roman Catholic in Practice*. Because of this, it is often seen as a bridge church and becomes a home for those looking for elements of both traditions in their community of faith.

The boundaries and contours of this mixing of Protestantism and Roman Catholicism have led to a variety of styles and approaches within the tradition. Traditionally, the three most significant are *Low Church, High Church*, and *Broad Church*. At the two ends of the spectrum are those churches that emphasize Protestant or Roman Catholic elements.[3] The Broad church tradition includes both elements.

Anglicanism's faith is founded in the scriptures, the traditions of the church, the "historic episcopate," and the use of reason, scholarship, and human experience.

Of these, the first and foremost is the Bible, which Anglicans feel contain all that is necessary for salvation. They use the Apostles' and Nicene Creeds regularly in worship and base what they believe on a literal or figurative interpretation of them and the *Thirty-Nine Articles of Religion*, early community documents that state basic Anglican beliefs and practices. Anglicans believe that the Apocrypha is an important set of documents. However, they see them as having less authority than the Bible. They may be read in church services as scripture, but when done, the *Celebrant* (i.e., the term for the officiating pastor or priest) typically will make a statement that the Apocrypha is profitable to read, but is not scripture.

In the United States, Canada, and Great Britain, Anglicans are culture-affirming and rank generally at the top of the socio-economic ladder, even higher than Presbyterians. They are generally highly educated and are leaders in their communities. In the rest of Anglicanism, the average believer is female, black, poor, and uneducated.

---

[3] Low Church advocates prefer Morning and Evening Prayer as opposed to Holy Communion services. Some use free-form services instead of Prayer book ones. Low Churches also incorporate elements of charismatic Christianity. An example of the former is the Diocese of Sydney and the latter, the so-called "Happy-Clappy" churches in Great Britain. Ministers may or may not be called priests. There is a stress on the Bible over the traditions of the church. Bishops are seen more as administrators than pastors. Ministers more often are named "Mr." or are called by their first name. Saints and the universal nature of the church are downplayed.

Those who choose High Churchmanship choose to focus on the importance of regular participation in the Eucharist, which they may call the Mass. Pastors are called priests and incense and sanctus bells may be employed in worship. Eucharistic adoration and the use of rosaries may be found. An emphasis on saints and the universal or Catholic institution of the church and the pastoral role of the bishop are also parts of this approach.

Broad Church (sometimes labeled Latitudinarianism) individuals call for a greater mixture of low and high church elements in belief, worship, and institution views. They refuse to take the label of the other two parties.

Anglican worship is liturgical and highly dramatic. Typically, churches have robed choirs and organs. In services, participants "kneel to prayer, stand to sing and sit to listen."

The church uses its *Book of Common Prayer*, which contains rubrics or directions for worship services. Although the first version of the *Book of Common Prayer* was created in 1549 CE by Thomas Cranmer, it has undergone many revisions. Also, some Anglican churches in different nations have developed their own versions of the book. Still, it may be argued that one of the major unifying aspects of international Anglicanism is the *Book of Common Prayer*.

However, even though the prayer book is followed, churchmanship determines the emphases of a particular service. In a Low Church, focus is on the sermon with Bible readings, prayers, and hymns. In a High Church, there is normally a more formal liturgy, not unlike a Roman Catholic service or at least a Pre-Vatican II service without the Latin.

For Anglicans, sacraments are believed to be "outward and visible signs of inward and spiritual grace." In these sacraments, grace is transmitted to the recipient.

Baptism and Holy Communion are two sacraments that Anglicans believe were instituted by Christ. Depending on the churchmanship, Anglicans may add five more. These may be seen as full sacraments or as lesser rites. If included, they are same ones as found in Roman Catholicism (except clergy may marry).[4]

Anglicans baptize all ages by sprinkling, which usually means an infant. Adults may be sprinkled or immersed, although immersion is rare. They believe that it is not necessary to repeat this ritual. Anglicans accept the baptisms of other traditions if they are valid.

Holy Communion may also be called the Eucharist or the Lord's Supper in this community of faith. They normally use crackers or bread and wine. In recent years, Anglicans of all stripes have begun to follow the lead of High Church advocates by having communion once a week during the main worship service.

Anglicans disagree about what exactly occurs in the spiritual realm in the service. Some believe that in the Lord's Supper, the elements remain exactly as they are, bread and wine. Others maintain that Christ is present in the elements (i.e. the Real Presence) or that the bread and wine become the body and blood of Christ (i.e., Transubstantiation).

In many ways, Anglicans appear to appreciate that what actually occurs in the Lord's Supper is a mystery. To make this point, both are stated in the *Book of Common Prayer*.

Take eat: This is my body, which is given for you. Do this for the remembrance of me . . . Drink this, all of you: This is my Blood of the new

---

[4] Confession, Marriage, Confirmation, Holy Orders, Anointing of the Sick.

Covenant, which is shed for you and for many for the forgiveness of sins. Whenever you drink it, do this for the remembrance of me.[5]

Anglicans have saints that have days set aside for them, as well as churches and children that are named for them. A few Anglicans pray to these saints like their Roman Catholic counterparts.

Wherever the British Empire spread during the 18th through 20th centuries CE, Anglican churches were founded first for British citizens and second for converts from colonial areas by the "Mother" church, *The Church of England.*

Today, there are 75 million Anglicans in the worldwide *Anglican Communion*, a term of relatively recent origin for the communion. This community has 44 member churches. Of these, 2-3 million are in the United States. The largest groups are in Africa; namely Nigeria, the Sudan, Kenya, and Uganda.

Churches throughout the world are each autonomous. They are mostly based on national identity (i.e., the English, Nigerian, and Cuban Anglican churches). Chief bishops direct these churches and have different titles, such as primate, archbishop, and presiding bishop.

The Anglican Church has religious orders for men and women.

In many locations, Anglicanism's geographic divisions have broken down. Instead, in a given location, churches may be affiliated with different chief bishops, some of whom do not recognize each other. These "overlapping" jurisdictions are of great concern to some of the oldest and largest groups.[6]

The Anglican Communion has no international groups or individuals that direct the movement. Instead, all international "instruments of unity" are consultative and collaborative: the every ten-year *Lambeth Conference*, the biennial *Anglican Consultative Council* (made up of lay and ordained representatives of the communion's churches), the Anglican Communion's *Primates Meetings* (i.e., chief bishops' meetings) and the *Archbishop of Canterbury.* No decisions made by these groups are considered binding on any part of the Communion.

For a vast majority of the world's Anglicans, the Archbishop of Canterbury is the head of the church in some fashion. Anglicans differ on whether groups have to be recognized by the Archbishop to be truly Anglican or if Anglicanism is defined by those churches with only "historic ties" to Canterbury.

The Archbishop of Canterbury is the chief bishop and principal leader of the Church of England, the symbolic head of the Anglican Communion and

---

[5] Oxford University Press, author, *The Book of Common Prayer and Administration of the Sacraments and Other Rites and Ceremonies in the Church*, Pew ed. edition (New York: Oxford University Press, 2001), pp. 362-363.

[6] Similar situations might be seen in the reactions of the large United States automakers complaining about the successes of Toyota and Nissan and the reactions of major airlines to popularity of Southwest Airlines. "Overlapping" jurisdictions are found in Anglicanism, Roman Catholicism, and Eastern Christianity.

the diocesan bishop of the See of Canterbury. He directs the most important international meetings of the church. The Archbishop is considered "first among equals." He serves for life unless he retires or resigns and he can be married.

The English crown is the *Supreme Governor* of the Church of England. This means that whoever holds this position has a role in appointing bishops and in particular, the Archbishop of Canterbury. While the crown legally has the right to choose the archbishop, the Prime Minister of Great Britain makes the selection in the name of the crown. The crown has no authority outside of England, Scotland, and Wales. However, in some places in the world, prayers for the crown are part of worship services. The close connection of church and state in Great Britain is one of the hallmarks of this branch of Christianity.

Anglicanism's leadership is located in bishop, priest, and deacon. The first are the chief pastor and administrators of local geographic areas called dioceses. They approve, ordain, and then help place candidates for ordained ministry in conjunction with local churches and diocesan committees. More often than not, local pastors, sometimes called presbyters or priests, lead local congregations. These local leaders have the authority to officiate the sacraments. Deacons are either priests-in-training or permanent deacons.

The largest American church, *The Episcopal Church (TEC)*, and a majority of international Anglican churches have women priests and some have women bishops.[7] For example, women priests can be found in the Churches of Uganda and Kenya, which have churches in North America.

In the United States, most, but not all, smaller offshoots do not, such as the Reformed Episcopal Church (a 19th century CE offshoot), the Continuing Churches (mostly churches that left over women's ordination in the 1970s CE and 1980s CE) and some recent Anglican movements in North American (i.e., the Anglican Missions in America).[8]

Until recently, the North American and European branches of the Anglican Communion have encouraged any sincere attempt to study and investigate religious matters. As a result, these branches have been havens for intellectual seekers and questioners. In this group, it has been acceptable to ask questions, even about the fundamentals of faith and having opposing opin-

---

[7] Women bishops can be found in the United States, New Zealand, Canada, Ireland, and Scotland.

[8] The Anglican Missions in America is an umbrella organization that includes two nations (United States of America and Canada) and two positions on the ordination of women. One of its subgroups, the Anglican Mission in America (AMiA), does not ordain women to the priesthood, but only to the deaconate. Two other subgroups, the Anglican Coalition of Canada (ACiC) and the Anglican Coalition in America (ACiA), ordain women to the priesthood and the deaconate.

ions has been honored. Because of this, there has been a wide range of views within the church and the ideal, "loyalty in essentials and liberty in non-essentials" has been held in high regard.

However, the debate in the North American and European sections of the Anglican world has been over what constitutes the essentials. The American branch adopted the position that traditional views on the authority of scriptures, key doctrines, and sexual ethics are not core essentials.

This approach has clashed with the approach taken by a vast majority of Anglicans, who believe that there are certain essentials one should believe to be an Anglican Christian, including sexual ethics, traditional views of the authority of scripture and key doctrines.

Until October 2003 CE, the Communion maintained a delicate balancing act between these opposing approaches. But, when the openly gay *Gene Robinson* was consecrated Bishop of New Hampshire, that ended. This recent global controversy (plus the debate over the blessing of same-sex marriages) has thrown the global Anglican community into turmoil and major schism. On the international level, the Communion adopted the *Windsor Report* (2004 CE) which states that marriage is for a man and woman only and practicing homosexuals cannot be ordained.

Up until this point sections of the Communion, primarily in the United States and Canadian churches, have paid "lip service" to the report while continuing to carry out actions contrary to it. On the other hand, a majority of the world's Anglicans support the findings of the Windsor Report. Presently, they are working on a communion-wide covenant based on the Windsor Report. If adopted, member churches would have to affirm this document to be core members of Communion. However, many have decided that the Anglican Communion does not have the will to support the premises of the Windsor Report and/or the covenant. The current Archbishop of Canterbury's inaction or as some suggest, outright stifling of the goals of the Report, has not helped resolve the crisis.

## Methodist

This umbrella term refers to those Protestant Christians who have their roots in the ministry of two Church of England clergy, *John Wesley* and his brother *Charles*. The following are highly prized by Methodists:

- John Wesley:  The English priest who is considered to be the founder of worldwide Methodism.

- The Wesleyan Quadrilateral:  Coined by Albert Outler in the 20$^{th}$ century CE, this refers to the belief that there are four sources for religious truth: the Bible (the Old and New Testaments), tradition (2,000 years of Christian teaching and practice), reason (rational thinking and sensible interpretation) and experience (a Christian's personal journey with Christ).[9]

- **The Bible:** Methodists hold the Bible to be the final authority in the Quadrilateral. Yet, they have a great deal of flexibility when it comes to Bible interpretation.

- **Secondary Authorities:** Methodists add to the Bible, secondary things such as Christian tradition (especially their roots in the Church of England), reason and experience.

- **Wesleyan Arminianism:** Influenced by Dutch theologian Jacob Arminius, Wesley's version argued for free will, anyone can be saved, resistible and prevenient grace, unlimited atonement, an ability to lose one's salvation, and perfectionism. At the same time, Wesley believed in original sin and the need for God's initiated grace in salvation.

- **Perfectionism:** Wesley taught that humans can be "perfect in love." This does not mean "sinless perfection," but it refers to a change of inner motive so a person can intentionally decide not to sin.

- **Small Groups:** The method of Methodism.

- **Social Action:** Methodists emphasize transforming individuals and society. They have been heavily involved in abolitionism, temperance, and feminism.

In the 1700s CE, the Wesleys were profoundly disturbed by the lack of spiritual vitality they found in their Anglican church. To counteract these issues, the Wesleys employed a method to revitalize Christians—*the Small Group*. These groups sought to encourage individuals in their spiritual life and to help the needy.

The term "Methodist" was a pejorative title given to a group of men who met at Oxford from 1729-1735 CE who carried out this project along with Bible study. These men studied the Bible, received weekly communion, agreed to abstain from what they perceived to be worldly amusements and visited the poor and sick.

---

[9] See Albert C. Outler, ed, *John Wesley* (Oxford: Oxford University Press, 1964).

For many years, Methodism was merely a subgroup of Anglicanism in England. Participants might attend the Anglican church on Sunday morning and Methodist meetings on Sunday evenings or during the week.

In the beginning, Methodism drew from all social classes, but because of its missionary efforts it began to have a sizable impact on working class individuals. Coupled with this was Wesley's use of street corner preaching, which attracted people who had little connection with organized religion. Wherever Methodists went, they preached (on street corners and in fields), established societies (which had classes or small groups), and held love feasts, which included the telling of personal testimonies.

The link between Anglicans and Methodists broke down when John Wesley ordained leaders for his movement outside of the Anglican Church. He approved men and women as lay preachers in 1739 CE and then ordained preachers for Scotland, the Americas, and England in 1784 CE.[10] Wesley felt that he had waited long enough for the Bishop of London to provide sacraments from duly ordained individuals for the growing ranks of Methodists in America. With the step, Wesley acted like a de-facto bishop, even though he was an Anglican pastor.

Before the end of the 1700s CE, Methodism became established as an independent entity in Great Britain and North America. Today, it attracts individuals from all levels of society. The largest branch of Methodism is the United Methodist Church with an approximate membership of 12 million throughout the world.

The most important focus of Methodist theology is how the grace of God operates in the individual and in society. This comes in three notions: *Prevenient Grace*, *Justifying Grace*, and *Sanctifying Grace*. Prevenient grace or the "grace that goes before" is provided to all people. This form of grace gives individuals the capacity to choose to bring Jesus Christ into their lives. Justifying or accepting grace cancels guilt and provides acceptance and forgiveness for the repentant soul. This may be called the new birth or conversion. It may take place in a single moment or over a person's lifetime. Sanctifying grace empowers believers as they move toward "perfection of love."

Methodism believes that each human has free will to accept or reject the Gospel. Salvation can also be lost. To maintain one's saved state, the believer needs to continue in their relationship with Jesus Christ.

True to the Wesleys, Methodism emphasizes how life is lived first as opposed to what proper belief first.

Methodist lifestyle varies from group to group. Some smaller groups ban alcohol and movies and prescribe clothing styles for women. Because of their activist focus, Methodists are usually involved in social activism. They have a history of advocating women's rights and the rights of slaves to be free.

---

[10] Wesley ordained Dr. Thomas Coker (as superintendent of all Methodists in America) and Richard Whatcoat and Thomas Vasey (as ministers in America).

The wide latitude of Methodist views of social issues was demonstrated in the late twentieth century when Oral Roberts, a Pentecostal preacher and supporter of the Religious Right, and Hillary Rodham Clinton, a political figure and supporter of the Religious Left were both members of the United Methodist Church.[11]

Typical of the variety found in Methodism is the varying ways that Methodists worship. They have a suggested order of worship, but as a non-liturgical church, they can choose to use or not use this order. This order of worship is modeled after Anglicanism's *Book of Common Prayer.*

Methodist worship ranges from a very formal almost liturgical form to an informal, folksy style. The popularity and use of Charles Wesley's hymns is a trademark of Methodism. Charles Wesley, John Wesley' brother, published over 5,500 hymns. Some of his most famous are "And Can It Be That I Should Gain," "Christ the Lord is Risen Today," "Come Thou Long-Expected Jesus," "Hark the Herald Angels Sing," "Rejoice the Lord is King," and "O For A Thousand Tongues to Sing."

Methodism has two sacraments: baptism and communion. According to Article Sixteen of the *Articles of Religion,* an official statement of American Methodism, these sacraments are "not only badges or tokens of Christian men's profession, but rather they are certain signs of grace, and God's good will toward us, by which he doth work invisibly in us, and doth not only quicken, but also strengthen and confirm, our faith in him."[12] Methodism rejects the additional sacraments of Roman and Eastern Christianity because they are not in the same category as baptism and communion and have "partly grown out of the corrupt following of the apostles."[13]

Baptism, for Methodists, is a sign of faith, regeneration, and the new birth. It is also a way that Christians are separated from others that are not baptized. While Methodists baptize all ages by sprinkling, pouring, and im-

---

[11] For more information on the Religious Right, see "Fundamentalism," in Chapter Eleven.

The Religious Left is composed of individuals who advocate leftist political beliefs within the Christian tradition. As opposed to the Religious Right, under the guise of "social justice," this movement espouses government solutions, not private solutions, to the problems of healthcare (i.e., universal or socialized medicine), the poor and needy (i.e., expanded expenditures for welfare), and education (i.e., anti-school choice). Christian Leftists generally argue against increase government spending for the military and against the use of the United States military overseas (i.e., Iraq). The Christian Left is pro-abortion and supports homosexual marriage. Representatives of the American Christian Left include: Cornel West, John Howard Yoder, John Shelby Spong, Philip and Daniel Berrigan, Cindy Sheehan, Jeremiah Wright, Jim Wallis, Ron Sider, Barry W. Lynn, and Tony Campolo. *Sojourners Magazine* publishes from the Christian Left position.

[12] http://archives.umc.org/interior.asp?ptid=1&mid=1651

[13] http://archives.umc.org/interior.asp?ptid=1&mid=1651

mersion, they baptize mostly infants. They also have baby dedication services and then celebrate believers' baptism. They accept the baptisms of any Christian if it was performed in the name of the Father, Son, and Holy Ghost.

Methodists use bread/crackers and grape juice/wine in communion and believe that Christ is spiritually present in the elements in a "spiritual and heavenly manner." They reject the idea that the substance of the elements changes (i.e., transubstantiation). Methodists practice open communion and may take it weekly or monthly.

*Covenant Services* are popular among Methodists. Churches and individuals follow John Wesley's challenge to renew their covenants with God. Local communities hold annual covenant services on the first convenient Sunday of the year. During these activities, Wesley's Covenant Prayer may still be used.

An important season of the religious year for American Methodists is called *Kingdomtide*, the last 13 weeks before Advent. During this season, service to the poor is emphasized.

Methodist organization is based on *Connectionalism*. The concept here is that no faith community is an end to itself. Instead, each local group is "connected" to others in ever-widening circles and levels of authority. This is all based on Wesley's originally classes, societies, and annual conferences.

The United Methodist Church structure typifies this connectionalism. Several key terms mark this structure:

- Conference
- Council of Bishops
- Judicial Council
- Bishop
- Elder and Deacon

There are several levels of *Conferences* in the United Methodist Church. The highest, the General Conference, meets every four years and speaks for the church as a whole. The second level includes Jurisdictional and Central Conferences, which also meet every four years. The United States has five Jurisdictions and there are seven Central Conferences. The primary purpose of these meetings is to elect bishops, the chief administrators of the church.

In between these meetings, the Council of Bishops runs the church.

The Judicial Council is the highest court in the denomination. It interprets church law and passes judgment on whether church officials, churches, or conferences have obeyed it.

The *Annual Conference* comprises churches in a local area. It meets annually. Local clergy are members of this group, not their local church, if they have one.

Annual conferences are divided into districts led by District Superintendents. They assist the bishop in dealing with non-spiritual and spiritual concerns.

The United Methodist Church has no official headquarters, although many of its largest administrative offices are located in Nashville, Tennessee near Vanderbilt University (Vanderbilt has historic ties to the Methodist Church, but it is an independent institution). These offices cannot speak for the church as a whole, but they direct specific ministries, such as the General Board of Discipleship and the United Methodist Publishing House.

Clergy include bishops, elders, and deacons. They can be married, single, or divorced. Depending on the denomination, they can be male or female (for example, the United Methodist Church has had women clergy since 1956 CE). They are ordained as elders or deacons by bishops and then they are assigned to different ministries.

Bishops are quite powerful in the Methodist system. Bishops serve Episcopal areas, which can have one or more annual conferences. Candidates for bishops are found among the elders of the church. They run annual conferences and ordain elders and deacons.

Elders generally serve as local pastors and have authority to officiate the sacraments. They are part of the *Itinerating Ministry* and are under the authority of bishops. The term itinerating is derived from the early history of Methodism when preachers would travel from church to church or itinerate. In doing this, they often served more than one church at a time. All clergy appointments are decided annually by the bishop with the agreement of the annual conference cabinet. Until the bishop announces the list of appointments at the local annual conference, no appointment is established. Appointments are made for one year, but it is common for them to last for several years.

Deacons carry out ministries of service, such as musicians, liturgists and business administrators. They are generally assigned to one church by the bishop and do not itinerate. However, a deacon may have a ministry outside the local church.

Local Methodist churches are governed by an administrative council or board made up of lay members of the faith community. Elders sit on the board also.

Eighty percent of Methodists in the United States belong to the United Methodist Church (8 million+). The other 20% belong to a variety of more conservative groups, such as the Free Methodists, and there are some sizable Afro-American churches, such as the African Methodist Episcopal Church.

Almost all Methodist-related denominations (approximately 76 groups from 132 nations representing 70 million people) belong to the World Methodist Council located at Lake Junaluska, North Carolina, Nashville, Tennessee, and Atlanta, Georgia.

### Presbyterian

This umbrella term refers to churches that have the following key terms:

- John Calvin:     Founder of the movement which bears his name.

- John Knox:      Early leader of Scottish Presbyterianism.

- Westminster      Drawn up in 1646 CE, this confession has be-
  Confession      come a standard of faith for many Presbyterian
  of Faith:      churches worldwide.

- Pneumatic      Presbyterian understanding of what transpires
  Presence:      during Holy Communion (for more, see later in
  this section).

- Elder:      Leader in the Presbyterian tradition.

- Session:      The name given for governing bodies of local
  churches.

- Presbytery:      The name given to the leadership team for a
  group of churches.

Presbyterianism is the creation of the movement founded by *John Knox*, a Scott, who was committed to the ideas of John Calvin.[14] The term "Presbyterian" is derived from the Koiné Geek term "presbuteros," meaning elder (see Acts 14:23, Acts 20:17, and Titus 1:5).

Presbyterianism is a confessional and creedal church, although there is a wide range of ideas as to what this means. Considerable debate swirls around the question: Does a local church or ordination candidate have to agree to a literal reading of the *Westminster Confession of Faith* or other standards, such as the *Larger* or *Shorter Catechisms*, the *Westminster Standards* or the *Book of Confessions?*

Because of this divergence, some Presbyterian churches continue to maintain theological ideas such as predestination and limited atonement, while others have deleted these.

Since education, hard work and economic success is honored, Presbyterians tend to be highly educated, more affluent and more influential than other Protestants (except Anglican/Episcopalians).

Presbyterians emphasize life-long learning and education. Active study of the scriptures, theological writings, and understanding contemporary cultural issues is important.

---

[14] Many Presbyterian Churches of European continental origin are called Reformed Churches. Presbyterians can be found in significant numbers in Scotland, the United States, Korea, Northern Ireland, South Africa, France, the Netherlands and Switzerland.

Learning for learning's sake is not the goal of Presbyterian education. Instead, Presbyterians are culture-affirming people and seek to make the world a better place. It is assumed that the faithful will involve themselves in social concerns and social change and in some denominations, evangelism.

Presbyterians believe that a viable church can be found where the "True Gospel is preached and the true sacraments are administered." Services are highly organized and orderly and they tend to focus on intellect more than on emotions. This being said, there is a great variety in worship style among Presbyterians. Some can be very evangelistic and others can be very liturgical. Most American Presbyterians have a semi-formal mixture of hymn singing, preaching, and congregational participation.

The central feature of a Presbyterian worship service is the *Sermon*, which is usually delivered by a well-educated clergy person called a teaching elder.

Presbyterians believe in two sacraments (baptism and communion). They are signs of Christ's presence that seal believers in Christ, renew their faith, and set them aside for service.[15] Specific details for baptism and communion are:

- Baptism:  Presbyterians baptize infants or non-baptized adults by sprinkling (aspersion) or pouring (affusion). Both believers and their children are part of God's covenant and should be baptized. The baptism of children testifies to the belief that God's love claims people before they are able to respond in faith. Presbyterians accept the baptisms from other churches.

- Communion or the Lord's Supper:  Presbyterians use grape juice and crackers which are passed around to the faithful as part of the Sunday morning worship service. Communion is normally held once a month. Presbyterians believe in the Pneumatic or Spiritual Presence. This means that Christ via the Holy Spirit is present in the room while the community celebrates the Lord's Supper. The community is transformed or "transubstantiated" itself and the faithful are lifted up to heaven to feast with Christ. The Presbyterian reference to the "presence" does not mean the Christ is in the elements.

---

[15] http://www.pcusa.org/101/101-sacrament.htm

Presbyterianism has connectional government and is probably the best example of this style. This means that there are several levels of authority working in tandem. The method is conciliar, with each group theoretically advising and holding accountable each group lower on the rungs of authority.

Local churches are directed by *Teaching* and *Ruling Elders* through *Sessions* or *Consistories*.

Teaching elders are normally called pastors and they are responsible for teaching, worship, and conducting sacraments. These pastors are called by individual congregations. A local call must be approved by the local association of Presbyterians, called a *Presbytery* or *Classis*.

Ruling elders, laymen and/or women, are elected by the local congregation and ordained to serve. They assist the teaching elders and have responsibility for the nurture and leadership of the congregation. In large congregations, a Deacon Board (or Board of Directors, Diaconate or Deacon's Court) handles the buildings, finance, and ministry to the needy.

The next level of Presbyterian authority is the presbytery or classis, which has the responsibility for oversight of congregations in a local area. Each presbytery is composed of teaching and ruling elders from each congregation. It may also include retired ministers and local theological college professors. The officers of the presbytery are moderator and clerk. The former is the chair, the latter the group's secretary. The presbytery has to approve the ordination and calling of pastors.

Presbyteries send representatives to regional and national assemblies, sometimes called general assemblies, the next levels of authority in the Presbyterian system. In some groups, the synod is a group positioned between the presbytery and the general assembly. The leader of a general assembly is a moderator, who is assisted by a clerk and a deputy clerk.

The session-consistory/presbytery/synod/general assembly form of church governance is practiced by several other churches besides Presbyterian and Reformed groups.

In the United States, there are 2-3 million Presbyterians. The largest group is the Presbyterian Church (PC(USA)). Other prominent communities of faith include: the Presbyterian Church in America, the Orthodox Presbyterian Church, the Evangelical Presbyterian Church, the Reformed Presbyterian Church, the Bible Presbyterian Church, the Associate Reformed Presbyterian Church (ARP), the Cumberland Presbyterian Church, the Westminster Presbyterian Church in the United States (WPCUS), and the Reformed Presbyterian Church in the United States (RPCUS). The largest concentration of Presbyterians can be found around Charlotte, North Carolina and Pittsburgh, Pennsylvania.

On the international front, Presbyterians are members of the conservative World Reformed Fellowship (40 denominations, 68 local churches, and 339 individuals) and or the more liberal World Alliance of Reformed Churches or the WARC (214 denominations and churches in 107 nations).

an denominations divide over the question of the role of women as
ed teaching and ruling elders. The Presbyterian Church (USA), the
d Presbyterian Church and the Evangelical Presbyterian Church
᎑᎑᎑ women to these roles. The Presbyterian Church in America does not.

## Baptist

The largest of the five umbrella terms, Baptist, refers to individuals and
churches throughout the world that are marked by four freedoms:

- Soul Freedom:    Individuals can and should live their Christian
  lives without the influence or coercion of a
  higher church body.

- Bible Freedom:    Individuals have the right to interpret the Bible
  for themselves.

- Church
  Freedom:    Each local church has the right to govern itself
  without outside interference.

- Religious
  Freedom:    Each individual has the right to practice religion
  or not to practice religion. Also, there should
  be a separation of church and state.

Baptists track their roots back partially to the Anabaptists of the Reformation
Period. They are also descendents of the other three founding Protestant
movements. In the United States, Roger Williams or Dr. John Clarke are
credited with founding the first Baptist church in Rhode Island, in Provi-
dence and Newport respectively, in the 1600s CE.

Baptists have no designated statement of faith that members must adhere
to. They believe that the entire Bible (minus the Apocrypha) is the inspired
Word of God and that is it the sole authority for matters of faith and practice.

Members of Baptist churches believe in *Soul Freedom* (or Soul Liberty,
Freedom of Conscience or Soul Competency). This concept refers to the idea
that each individual has the God-given capacity and responsibility to make
choices about life and faith. No institution or hierarchy can do this for them.

Coupled with this is Luther's notion of priesthood of all believers. Each
person can access God as individuals without the necessity or assistance of a
church institution.

Although there is considerable variety among Baptist lifestyle choices, as
a whole, Baptists tend to set stricter standards about personal morality than
other Protestants. These guidelines govern the use of alcohol, going to movies, dancing, and playing cards.

Because they believe in *Religious Freedom*, Baptists advocate the right to practice religion or not to practice religion. They are strong advocates of the separation of church and state. This belief stems from the fact that Baptists trace their heritage back to the Anabaptists of the Reformation Era. At that time, the Anabaptists were the only major Reformation group that argued for this idea. The other three (Lutheran, Calvinist, and Anglican) all maintained close associations with their secular governments.

In recent years, Baptists have "come out of the closet" and have become involved heavily and publically in the political process in the United States. Jerry Falwell, who labeled himself proudly as a public Baptist, was a prime example of the new highly visible and activist form of Baptists.[16]

Baptist churches are non-liturgical, although many worship practices remain the same each week. The difference between their repetitive, non-liturgical practice and the practice of liturgical churches, such as Episcopalians and Lutherans, is that Baptists have control over and can change worship practices at the local level. The other churches have higher boards and commissions that are commissioned to alter religious practices.

Two ordinances, Baptism and the Lord's Supper, are practiced in Baptist worship. These are called ordinances because they are ceremonies that symbolize grace already given.

Baptism of those old enough to believe in Christ for themselves by total immersion is the first ordinance. This ritual is called *Believers' Baptism*. The movement rejects infant baptism. Instead, it teaches that a person has had to reach the Age of Accountability and has to have personal faith prior to baptism. While what is considered the Age of Accountability varies, it normally ranges from ages 8-15 years. Baptists will normally require those baptized as infants to be re-baptized. Baptisms are usually carried out during the main worship service. They can occur in a tank inside the local church, in a creek, or in a pond.

Baptism is typically done by full immersion to demonstrate a person's death to their old life and entrance into their new life. Baptists also believe that they should do as they believe John the Baptist did when used full immersion to baptize Jesus in the Gospels.[17]

To be a member of a Baptist congregation, in most cases, a person has to have been baptized. Some Baptists permit a person to join their local church with a declaration of faith or a letter of transfer from another Baptist or non-Baptist church. To admit individuals to church membership without believers' baptism has become a standard practice in certain places, but it is a minority and arguably a controversial position.

Crackers and grape juice are usually used in the second ordinance, the *Lord's Supper*. Baptists do not believe that Christ is present in the crackers and

---

[16] For more information on Jerry Falwell, see Chapter Eleven.

[17] See Matthew 3:13-17, Mark 1:9-11, and Luke 3:21-22 and possibly John 1:29-34.

grape juice. They remain in their seats when taking the Lord' Supper. These communities practice either open or closed communion. The Lord's Supper may take place weekly, monthly, quarterly, or annually. Usually the ritual occurs during the main worship service.

Besides these two ordinances, Baptist churches practice other rituals. Instead of infant baptism, they hold *Baby Dedications*. A newborn is normally brought with their parent(s) to the front of the church during the main worship service. At this point, the parents give their child to Jesus Christ and promise to raise that person in the faith and members of the congregation promise to lend their support.[18] A few Baptists added foot-washing (Free Will and Primitive Baptists) and/or a holy kiss on the cheek of a member of the same sex (Missionary).

Baptist communities of faith are part of the *Free Church Movement*. This movement maintains that each individual congregation is independent and can decide faith and practice issues for itself without the interference of hierarchical authorities.

Because each church is totally free to do as it pleases based on the will of its membership, there is a wide range of belief and practice among Baptist communities of faith. Some communities only use the King James Version of the Bible, while others use a variety of translations. There are also "bapticostal" Baptists, who combine Baptist and Pentecostal practices.[19] Some Baptists believe that the Sabbath should be on Saturday instead of Sunday.

Because of sheer numbers, Southern Baptists are usually touted as the prime example of congregational church government in any discussion of church governance. However, they may not be the best representatives of this form of church government because groups within the denomination have recently attempted to dictate local church policy.

For example, the denomination has expelled churches for ordaining and marrying practicing homosexuals.[20] Also, Southern Baptist churches on the national level have stated that wives are supposed to be submissive to their husbands and that churches should have an all-male pastorate to the denomination's statement of faith, the *Baptist Faith and Message*.[21]

---

[18] In one baby dedication ceremony, a promise "not to meddle" in the child's upbringing has been added.

[19] See Pentecostals in Chapter Twelve.

[20] See "North Carolina Baptists Expel Charlotte Church for Accepting Gays," http://www.abpnews.com/content/view/2968/120/

[21] The latest revision contains the following statements about these two issues: "The husband and wife are of equal worth before God, since both are created in God's image. The marriage relationship models the way God relates to his people. A husband is to love his wife as Christ loved the church. He has the God-given responsibility to provide for, to protect, and to lead his family. A wife is to submit herself graciously to the servant leadership of her husband even as the church willingly submits to the headship of Christ. She, being in the image of God as is her husband and

In response, in November 2003 CE, the Illinois Baptist Convention joined several other state associations and rejected these statements. This was done because Illinois Baptists did not wish to "violate the long-held Baptist beliefs of soul competency and local-church autonomy."

Although all power resides in local congregations, Baptist churches group together in local, state, national, and international organizations. As an example, Southern Baptists have local associations, and state and national conventions.

The two most important professional leaders in Baptist communities are *Pastors* and *Deacons* (and possibly deaconesses). Individuals who hold these positions may be male or female, depending on guidelines set by a local church or in some cases, by the denomination. Pastors normally come from outside the local community. They are hired or "called" by the vote of the entire church after the person "candidates" (i.e., visits the church and preaches). The candidate then leaves and every member of the church is eligible to vote for or against the person. Increasingly, Baptists churches require a seminary education.

Deacons assist the pastor by normally taking care of the needs of a local church. These include building and grounds care and budgetary concerns. Sometimes deacons assist with the spiritual care of members of the community. Normally, deacons come from inside the local church.

Youth pastors for school-age and college-age individuals and Christian education ministers or directors may assist pastors and deacons if the local church is large enough.

In the United States, approximately one in five Christians are Baptist and are members of 50+ groups. The largest communities of faith in the United States are:

- The Southern Baptist Convention
- The National Baptist Convention, USA, Inc.
- The National Baptist Convention of America, Inc.
- American Baptist Churches in the USA
- Baptist Bible Fellowship International[22]

---

thus equal to him, has the God-given responsibility to respect her husband and to serve as his helper in managing the household and nurturing the next generation" (Article 18).; "While both men and women are gifted for service in the church, the office of pastor is limited to men as qualified by Scripture" (Article 6). See *Baptist Faith and Message* (2008).

[22] Albert W. Wardin, *Baptists Around the World* (Nashville: Broadman and Holman Publishers, 1995), p. 367.

Baptists are found on every continent and number approximately 110 million members.[23] The Baptist World Alliance represents Baptist interests on the international level.

## Lutheran

Several key terms mark this umbrella term:

- Martin Luther: The German reformer who launched the Lutheran movement.

- The "Alones": Bible alone, faith alone, and grace alone.

- Law and Gospel: A balance of the two marks the Christian faith.

- Creeds: Lutheranism adheres to and uses several creeds.

- *Book of Concord* (1580 CE): A book that contains ten creedal statements accepted by Lutherans.

- Sacramental Union: Christ's body and blood are present in the bread and wine, but the bread and wine do not become the body and blood of Christ (as in Transubstantiation).

- Lifelong Learning: Members are encouraged to seek educational opportunities from the church and secular institutions throughout their lives.

- Two-Kingdom Theory: Two kingdoms, the secular and the spiritual, exist with separate God-defined responsibilities.

- Roster: The name given to the official list of ordained, commissioned, or consecrated individuals in the ELCA.

- Synod: Geographic divisions within the ELCA.

- Presiding Bishop: Chief pastor and executive of the ELCA.

---

[23] See the Baptist World Alliance for recent statistics at http://www.bwanet .org/default.aspx?pid=437

Lutheranism is that branch of Protestantism that follows the principles set forth by Martin Luther. This heritage is quite important to Lutherans.

Lutheranism is different than the Reformed (i.e., Presbyterian) churches of the Protestant Reformation because it, like Anglicanism, retained the sacrament and liturgical format of Roman Catholicism.

Published in 1580 CE, *The Book of Concord* is the historical doctrinal standard for Lutheranism. It contains ten creedal statements recognized as authorities in the tradition.[24] Of these, the Augsburg Confession of 1530 CE is of particular importance.

There is disagreement over whether Lutherans have to subscribe to these understandings or have to view them as important historical guides to the doctrines of the church.

Lutherans believe that the Bible is the written Word of God. It is inspired, authoritative, and the norm for faith and practice. Members of Lutheran groups do not agree on what inspiration, authoritative, and norm actually mean, however.

The Apocrypha is seen as an important document, but without the same authority as the Bible itself.

The Bible contains two different sets of content: *Law* and *Gospel* (or Law and Promises). The former calls for obedience to the law as a means of God's acceptance, while the latter provides forgiveness of sins through the person and work of Jesus Christ. As Martin Luther himself stated:

All Scripture ought to be distributed into these two principal topics, the Law and the promises. For in some places it presents the Law, and in others the promise concerning Christ, namely, either when [in the Old Testament] it promises that Christ will come, and offers, for His sake, the remission of sins justification, and life eternal, or when, in the Gospel [in the New Testament], Christ Himself, since He has appeared, promises the remission of sins, justification, and life eternal.[25]

Lutheranism teaches the "alones" or "onlys": Bible, faith, and grace alone. By these terms, the community means that salvation does not come through human works or the action of the church, but through Jesus Christ, God's grace (power to forgive and save), personal faith, and the Bible.

---

[24] The ten are: three early Christian creeds (The Apostles', Nicene, and Athanasian Creeds), the Augsburg Confession (1530), the Apology of the Augsburg Confession (1531), the Smalcald Articles (1537), Treatise on the Power and Primacy of the Pope (1537), The Smaller Catechism of Martin Luther (1529), The Larger Catechism of Martin Luther (1529), and The Formula of Concord (1577).

[25] Martin Luther, *Apology of the Augsburg Confession*, Article 4 (1531).

A corollary to the "alones," is Lutheranism's focus on the *Theology of the Cross*. First coined by Luther himself, "Theologia Crucis" maintains that the only way to know God and his plan for salvation is through the cross of Jesus Christ. This is in opposition of the *Theology of Glory* (i.e., "Theologia Gloriae"), which stresses the use of human reason and human abilities as a way to know God and his plan for salvation.

Because Lutherans believe that right living comes from right knowledge, they emphasize *Lifelong Education*. They assume that sound learning will change how people live.

The Lutheran emphasis on education has been demonstrated by the development of Lutheran schools on all levels of education and the interest Lutherans have in academics both inside and outside the church community. Lutherans have established a parochial school system in the United States, which is second in size to the Roman Catholic school system.

From its founding days, Lutheranism has emphasized the close connection of church and state. This is based on Martin Luther's Two-Kingdom Theory. Simply stated, Luther argued that God works in the world through two kingdoms operating with two sets of guidelines. The spiritual kingdom (i.e., the church) is made up of individuals who have experienced God's grace and who operate with faith and love. The earthly kingdom (i.e., secular governments) operates by the law through the sword and compulsion with the goal of maintaining order and peace. Even in those nations where Lutheranism is the state church today, this idea of different vocations stands.

Lutheran worship is liturgical. The orderly main service is a modified version of Luther's liturgy, which is a modified version of the Roman Catholic liturgy. The service consists of prayers, readings, a sermon, and communion. Lutherans enjoy the robust singing of Luther's own hymns. Lutherans see the altar of communion and the pulpit for preaching as equally important. God is present in each.

Lutheranism uses the term sacrament to describe their two most important rituals, baptism and communion. According to the Augsburg Confession, a sacrament not only gives grace to those experiencing the ritual, it also:

- Is a mark of Christian profession
- Is a sign and testimony of the will of God toward believers
- Was instituted to awaken and confirm faith in those who use them[26]

Baptism is a ritual associated with joining the Christian community and is commanded by God. According to the *Large Catechism*, baptism "snatches us

---

[26] ttp://www.iclnet.org/pub/resources/text/wittenberg/concord/web/augs013.html

from the jaws of the devil and makes God our own, overcomes and takes away sin and daily strengthens the new man."[27]

Although normally performed on infants, un-baptized adults may be baptized also. Baptism is normally done by sprinkling. Coupled with this, however, is the belief that an exact method is not required. Only the presence of the Word of God and water is mandated. Lutherans accept the baptisms of other Christians, if these baptisms were performed in the name of the Father, Son, and Holy Spirit.

In Holy Communion, the elements are the true body and blood of Christ "in, with and under the form" of the bread and wine for all those who eat and drink it. This is called the *Sacramental Union*.[28] Lutherans may use one of several terms for the service, such as the Lord's Supper, Communion, or the Eucharist. Communion may take place weekly, bi-weekly, or monthly.

Lutherans follow a yearly calendar of special days of remembrance. The most important celebration is weekly worship. Although there is an overall similarity of calendar schedules among different Lutheran groups, each group marks their own special days.

Because of the importance of Luther to Lutheranism, the *Festival of the Reformation* is celebrated each year on the Sunday closest to or before November 30. Worship includes singing, "A Mighty Fortress is our God," a hymn written by Luther himself. Lutherans normally stand when singing this song in memory of its use during the religious wars of the 16th century CE.

Lutheranism has a connectional form of church government. This is true even though its churches have bishops. The multi-level structure of this community of faith includes three main categories of local congregations, synods, and clergy. Lutheran groups have other individual ministries, such as being a deacon or deaconess, a military or college chaplain, or a director of Christian education, music, or youth.

An example is the Evangelical Lutheran Church in America (ELCA), the largest Lutheran group in North America. By constitution, this faith community is one body in three expressions: congregation, synod, and churchwide organization. These three share a common vision and provide leadership for the church.

The ELCA has 10,500 congregations in the United States, the Virgin Islands, and Puerto Rico. These communities of faith are led by pastors who are called by the local church. These individuals provide spiritual oversight and sacramental ministries. Although the bishop is involved in identifying potential candidates and affirming the selected person, it is ultimately the local church which makes the choice. This is done by vote of the congregation.

---

[27] http://www.lcms.org/graphics/assets/media/LCMS/wa_baptism.pdf
[28] Another term "consubstantiation" is used by some Lutheran groups. Other groups explicitly reject the use of the term.

The community has 65 synods. These are comprised of congregations within specific geographic areas. They provide a place for united effort, regional support, and for guiding pastoral and other candidates through the ordination process.

The *Churchwide Organization* works with congregations and synods to ensure that the ministry of the ELCA is carried out. This group is led by the Churchwide Assembly, the Church Council, the Conference of Bishops, and the four elected officers of the church (presiding bishop, treasurer, secretary, and vice-president).

A staff assists the Churchwide Organization from Lutheran Center in Chicago, Illinois and from other locations. Members of this group are administrators, advisors, conveners, and resource people.

The biennial *Churchwide Assembly* is the highest legislative body for the ELCA and it is responsible for directing the church. The assembly has clerical and lay members. It reviews the work of church officers, synods, and churchwide offices, establish budgets and churchwide policies and has the sole authority to alter constitutional provisions for the church.

The Church Council functions as the board of directors for the denomination between churchwide assemblies. This group is advised by the Conference of Bishops.

Bishops are elected by synods for six year terms of service and they can be reelected. Bishops are responsible for ordaining all pastors and approving the list or roster of all current pastors. They are called to uphold Luther's teachings.

In most Lutheran groups, bishops have not been in apostolic succession. A more developed hierarchical church system can be found today in Scandinavia, the Baltic countries, Russian, and some areas of Africa. After a 1999 CE Concordant with the Episcopal Church, ELCA Lutherans accepted the idea that all future ordinations (from 1999 CE) would be carried out in apostolic succession.

Bishops meet at least twice a year in the conference of bishops along with the presiding bishop and the ELCA secretary. Their role is primarily advisory, but they also are involved with issues involving rostered leaders, the ordination process, churchwide planning, and ecumenical relations. The Conference of Bishops also issues pastoral letters, such as "On the Current Financial Crisis" on October 7, 2008 CE.

The *Presiding Bishop* of the ELCA is elected to a four-year term by the churchwide assembly. In his ministry, this individual "wears many hats." The presiding bishop carries out the typical ministries of preacher, teacher, administrator of the sacraments and pastor.

Besides these, the Presiding Bishop is the church's president and chief executive officer. In this role, he handles staff, budget, and other administrative issues for the church as a whole. The presiding bishop chairs the Churchwide Assembly. This person establishes the plans for the assembly, the Church Council, the Conference of Bishops, and the cabinet of executives.

Lutheranism is one of the largest Protestant groups in the world with approximately 68 million members throughout the world.

The Lutheran Church is the state religion of Finland, Sweden, Denmark, Iceland, and Norway. It retains a huge influence in Germany, its place of origin where it once was the state religion.

The Lutheran tradition has several major and minor branches. The largest Lutheran group in North America is the Evangelical Lutheran Church in America with 4.8 million members in 1988 CE.[29] The second- and third-sized Lutheran groups are: the Lutheran Church—Missouri Synod (2.4 million members) and Wisconsin Evangelical Lutheran Synod (WELS, 400,000 members).

Globally, Lutherans are linked through several groups. The Lutheran World Federation (LWF), founded in 1947 CE, has one-hundred and forty member churches from 79 nations representing approximately 68.3 million members.[30] The International Lutheran Council (ILC) is a worldwide association of confessional Lutherans with 30 member churches and 3.4 million members.[31] The Confessional Evangelical Lutheran Conference (CELC) has 20 member churches.[32]

Lutheran groups are divided over whether ordained clergy have to be men only or both men and women and whether practicing homosexuals can be clergy. The largest American branch, the Evangelical Lutheran Church in America, has women pastors. A denominational task force has recently challenged the church to accept gay and lesbian pastors.[33] In the summer of 2009 CE, the ELCA Churchwide Assembly approved the ordination of practicing homosexuals and lesbians. Other groups, such as the LMS do not have women pastors nor do they approve gay or lesbian ones.

---

[29] http://www.lutheranworld.org/Directory/NAM/EvLuthCchinAmerica-EN.html
[30] http://www.lutheranworld.org/Who_We_Are/LWF-Welcome.html
[31] http://www.ilc-online.org/pages/default.asp?NavID=69
[32] http://www.celc.info/index.php
[33] "Released February 19 by an ELCA task force, the 'Proposed Social Statement on Human Sexuality' and related 'Rostering Recommendations' admit there is no consensus about how the Lutheran church should treat its gay members and pastors. The twenty page document recommends allowing churches and synods to make their own decisions on non-celibate gay pastors, a change from the current ban. But the document does not call for rites for blessing gay unions, nor does it call for the re-rostering of defrocked gay pastors."

### SEE WHAT YOU KNOW ABOUT THE FIVE UMBRELLA TERMS OF PROTESTANTISM

1. Identify and describe four beliefs.

2. Identify and describe three characteristics of lifestyle.

3. Identify and describe four characteristics of ceremonies.

4. Identify and describe three characteristics of institutions.

# APPENDIX
## ✠
# AN EASTERN CHRISTIAN TIMELINE OF CHURCH HISTORY

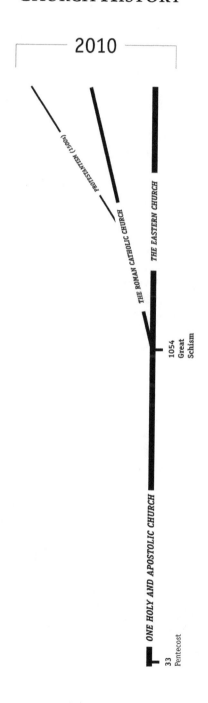

2010

PROTESTANTISM (1500s)

THE ROMAN CATHOLIC CHURCH

THE EASTERN CHURCH

1054
Great
Schism

ONE HOLY AND APOSTOLIC CHURCH

33
Pentecost